THE BROADVIEW BOOK OF

Canadian Anecdotes

THE BROADVIEW BOOK OF

Canadian Anecdotes

Edited by

Douglas Fetherling

broadview press

Canadian Cataloguing in Publication Data
  Main entry under title:
  The Broadview Book of Canadian Anecdotes
  ISBN 0-921149-29-8
  1. Canada — Biography — Anecdotes. I. Fetherling, Douglas, 1949- .
  II. Title: Canadian anecdotes.
  FC25.B76 1988   920'.071   C88-094572-9

broadview press   in the U.S.: broadview press
P.O. Box 1243   421 Center Street
Peterborough, Canada. K9J 7H5   Lewiston, N.Y. 14092

Printed and bound in Canada by
Gagné Ltd.

Contents

The Natural History of the Anecdote

There is a great proliferation of anecdote collections these days. Pessimists might accept this as further proof that the culture is becoming trivialized, as people's attention spans grow still shorter through the magic of video. Optimists, however, are free to interpret the trend differently. They can take it as another sign of our wide-ranging and abiding interest in the past. Specifically, they can view it in the fashionable context of social history, in which the lives of ordinary people, or the routine parts of the lives of extraordinary ones, are judged worth studying and learning from. I prefer to be among the optimists, but in choosing sides I'm conscious of the need to know something about the history of the anecdote and the anecdote as history.

The present vogue for anecdotes goes back to 1975 and the publication of *The Oxford Book of Literary Anecdotes* by James Sutherland. That collection, which established the format for all manner of subsequent ones, such as *The Oxford Book of Legal Anecdotes* and *The Oxford Book of Theatrical Anecdotes,* carried a now rather well known preface in which Sutherland charts the evolution of the very word "anecdote". He points out that Dr Johnson in his *Dictionary* of 1755 stuck with the Greek definition — "something yet unpublished; secret history" — but by the fourth edition of 1773 had loosened up, grudgingly to judge from Boswell's testimony. "It is now used, after the French, for a biographical incident; a minute passage of private life", he admitted.

Another way of showing the difference would be to remind ourselves that the reason we know Johnson's personality so well is that Boswell made such practical use of anecdotes as *belles lettres,* and that the story of the anecdote from that time to this has been its gradual acceptance by popular biographers. Significantly, though, the anecdote is not in the mainstream of professional historical writing and never has been. Livy wasn't doing the job of an anecdotalist, for he was at least as interested in identifying larger forces as in describing small deeds. The roots of the anecdote as we know it today are moral, religious and philosophical, and they come from both Roman and Greek soil.

The Roman anecdote seems to arise naturally from the twin facts that moral instruction was an essential part of the historian's art and that most of the historians, in fact most Roman prose writers of all types, were Stoics. Tacitus was more than an anecdotalist; he was perhaps closer to one of the later court essayists, given that what he says of princes and politicians is always a cut of mere anecdote. Yet the nature of the job and his lofty moral tone meant that there was an anecdotalist somewhere inside him. A clearer example is Hadrian's secretary Suetonius, the author of *The Lives of the First Twelve Caesars,* whose anecdotal structure was probably a major influence on many later books about rulers and also on Vasari's *Lives of the Artists.* Today, it is in campaign biographies and the sort of extended puffery that business executives commission about themselves so unselfconsciously that the Roman tradition is closest to the surface. The moral function may have atrophied, but what's left is the hagiographic, the suggestion that here, in a particular anecdote, the great man is brought right to the table, in his own words or at least a plausible reconstruction of them.

By way of contrast, the Greeks did not feel the same necessity to use history for moral lessons, to ensure that good triumph for the sake of the young. Greek history was a literary form, existing for its own sake, with its own muse no less. Anecdotes were important but largely as a stylistic device and yet they were less stylized in their function. They were more, in a word, informational— however selectively and to whatever ultimate purpose. In Hellenic culture then and much later, one of the writer's tasks was to show the people being written about in the best light, whether by anecdotes, sayings, or other means. Isn't that essentially what Luke was doing for Jesus when writing down what Jesus no doubt would have said in a particular situation?

Insofar as the Greeks are concerned, there are two great foundations of the written anecdote—to the purists, a contradiction in terms, I know. The one is *Lives of the Greek Philosophers* by Diogenes Laertius. The other is the *Anecdota* of Procopius, one of his two histories of the Justinian court. It was probably when the second of these was rediscovered and became known throughout Europe in the sixteenth century that the word "anecdote" began to lose its suggestion of secrecy and arcana and to take on the definition Dr Johnson acknowledged with such reluctance. Which is proof that the Greek tradition of anecdote outlasted the Roman. Certainly the Greek is the more important of the two as a basis of English ancedote and thus of our own as well. Sir Thomas More, to take one example, was not content to chronicle events in his *History of the Life and Death of King Edward V and of the usurpation of Richard III* but collected all the anecdotes he could, arranging them to suit his political purposes. Perhaps that's why Shakespeare found the work worth consulting.

For hundreds of years, anecdotes were the preserve of antiquarians, something to be plucked from ancient manuscripts, the way one sought pottery shards in barrows and geological specimens at promising hillsides. The Victorians too made a cult of the gifted amateur, and it was a reaction against the dilettantism around him that Sir Leslie Stephen, in *The Dictionary of National Biography*, dismissed John Aubrey as "certainly devoid of literary talent, except as a retailer of anecdote" (a judgement that the essayist Christopher Morley tried to soften, calling Aubrey a compiler of "biographical memoranda"). The word "anecdotes" was sometimes used interchangeably with "curiosities" in that now obsolete non-pejorative sense of that which is interesting because it is unusual even if not necessarily valuable: *bijoux* rather than sideshow attractions. So the stage was set for Samuel Smiles.

Smiles was a Scottish businessman who in 1859 published a self-help book called *Self-help,* a famous bestseller that spurred scores or hundreds of rivals, and has remained in print ever since. This simple collection of anecdotes about great men of the past and present, chosen for the purpose of teaching greatness to others or at least letting them identify it, was a book given to adolescents once they had graduated from G.A. Henty. It was intended to stiffen their upper lips and reinforce their commercial resolve. Smiles's practical hints for self-improvement could not boast of any moral underpinning in the philosophical sense (and no morals in the narrative sense). Still, the age of faith had not quite been supplanted by secular times, and the book did have some bearing on the question of ethics, to the extent that it promoted good conduct as the key to redemption. But from the literary point of view, the significance of Smiles, and it is great, is that his anecdotes were free-standing, grouped thematically but not in a forensic pattern or in any particular order within each category. From there it was only a short step to anecdotes in the more contemporary sense of the word: as self-supporting vignettes providing entertainment of a kind.

What began as moral teaching, then, became uncomplicated pedagogy and finally mere amusement. The meaning of the word, however, has continued to evolve, as can be shown using Canadian examples.

During the First World War, *Saturday Night* ran a department headed "Anecdotes". It was in fact the humour page, full of jokes, witticisms, and natty stories. The "Canadianecdotes", so called, that *Maclean's* began printing after the Second World War were quite different. They were observations, specimens of real-life wackiness and out-of-the-way information that existed if not always to amuse the subscribers then certainly to divert them. The idea was that by their revealing eccentricity or in some cases their poignancy or even their crystalizing pithiness, they would begin to highlight patterns in Canadian life. They had less in common with jokes than with those little slivers of self that Apollinaire called *anecdotiques*; despite their episodic, even fragmentary character, they showed that the trivial can be a serious matter. If taken in sufficient quantity, they might also be a celebration of Canada's social fabric. Such is the purpose of the following pages.

Putting together this collection has been an educational experience. One is conscious of the need to eschew any metaphor that turns on use of the word "mosaic", but in this case some phrase of that sort is needed. I have striven to avoid as much as possible anecdotes which are "apocryphal", another old Greek word, whose change in meaning parallels that of "ancedote"; I use it here in both the original sense ("of unknown authorship") and the modern sense ("untrue"). So I have drawn most often on published biographies, autobiographies and memoirs. Assuming, as it seems fair to do, that such books are a useful indication of eminence and success in our society, then it's truly extraordinary how few Canadian women were so honoured until the present generation, or how few native people are favoured with them even today. I have tried to acknowledge such imbalances when deciding what to include and what to omit, just I have attempted to present many less familiar anecdotes which have the virtue of freshness as well as piquancy.

You won't find here the story of the young John Diefenbaker selling a newspaper to Sir Wilfrid Laurier or of Morley Callaghan knocking down Ernest Hemingway in a boxing ring (though I couldn't resist Donald Smith's poor showing in driving the last spike of the Canadian Pacific). In place of those, I hope I have put a few surprises, not only in the stories themselves, but in what unexpected facts they reveal when arranged in the James Sutherland manner, in ascending order according to year of birth.

It seems perfectly plausible, in some impossible to articulate way, that Pierre Trudeau and Igor Gouzenko were born in the same year, given that their careers were different reactions to a single set of historical circumstances. But it strikes me as laughable that Stephen

Leacock was the same age, give or take a few months, as Oscar Wilde's friend Robbie Ross, or that R.B. Bennett and Emily Carr were right behind them. The circumstances that made Nellie McClung and Mackenzie King almost exact contemporaries aren't hard to grasp or appreciate. Yet the fact that they shared the distinction with Robert W. Service makes one shake one's head. When they lived, such people existed in separate little compartments; now that they're gone, anecdotes assist in breaking down the barriers and restoring organic relationships.

To say any more on the subject, however, would be to risk trafficking in anecdotes about anecdotes and therefore to miss the point, which is to encourage browsing in the well-stocked past.

Ed.

The Anecdotes

1
Samuel de Champlain (1567-1635)

On his first visit to Canada, in 1603, Champlain was introduced to the *tabagie* (in Quebec the word soon came to refer to a tobacconist's shop or convenience store but in Europe it retains its original meaning—feast). The Algonquins, who except for the painted designs on their bodies reminded Champlain of French beggars with heavy suntans, made diplomatic speeches and offered the foreigners "the flesh of moose, which is like beef, [along] with that of bear, seal, and beaver, which are their most ordinary meats, and with great quantities of wild fowl." Champlain was moved to remark on their general disregard of proper hygiene, particularly the custom of wiping greasy hands on the nearest dog.

Shortly afterwards Champlain was the guest at a celebration to mark a recent defeat of the Iroquois and saw still other curious and shocking customs. "They arranged all their women and girls side by side, and themselves stood behind, singing all in unison," he wrote. "Suddenly all the women and girls proceeded to cast off their mantles of skins, and stripped themselves naked, showing their privities, but retaining their ornaments of matachias, which are beads and braided cords made of porcupine quills, dyed of various colors. After they had made an end of their songs, they cried all with one voice: 'Ho, ho, ho!' At the same instant all the women and girls covered themselves with their mantles, which were at their feet, and they had a short rest; then all at once beginning again to sing, they let fall their mantles as before. They do not stir from one spot when they dance, but make certain gestures and motions of their body, first lifting up one foot and then the other, and stamping upon the ground.

"While they were performing this dance, the Sagamore ... was seated before the said women and girls, between two poles, on which hung the scalps of their enemies. Sometimes he arose and moved away to address [his allies] the Montagnais and Etchemins, saying to them: 'See how we rejoice for the victory which we have obtained over our enemies; ye must do the like, that we may be satisfied.' Then all cried together: 'Ho, ho, ho!' As soon as he had returned to his place, the Grand Sagamore and his companions cast off their mantles, being stark naked save for their privities, which were covered with a small piece of skin [whereupon the Montagnais and Etchemins revealed the gifts they had brought] such as matachias, tomahawks, swords, kettles, pieces of fat, moose flesh, seal; in a word, everyone had a present, which they proceeded to give to the Algonquins. After all these ceremonies the dance came to an end, and the Algonquins, both men and women, carried away their presents to their lodges. They also matched two of the fittest men of each nation, whom they caused to run, and he who was swiftest in the race had a present."

By 1637, the French priests had squelched such ceremonial nudity but in other respects the complicated war ritual continued.

2

Jeffrey Amherst, 1st Baron Amherst (1717-97)

The general whose capture of Louisbourg in 1758 made him British military commander of North America and one of the founders of modern Canada was credulous about the occult, to judge from this letter written by his sister, Elizabeth Amherst Thomas, to a clergyman friend.

"Reverend Sir

"I have a favor to beg of you. Can you give me any information about the belief in Germany concerning Vampers or Vampires? (I think they call them). When I mentioned that strange superstition to my brother Jeff, he assured me that it was undoubtedly true, as several officers of good reputation in the German army had solemnly protested that it was certainly so, and he had had to give up saying that he could not believe it, or they would have been highly offended...

"The German officers told my Brother that some particular families were liable to have their dead turn into Vampires, upon which some surviving relation would grow pale and sickly and slowly pine away. If this happened it became necessary to open the family vault, and examine the dead bodies, and when they found one that looked fresh and lively, they cut off its head. If it was a Vampire, fresh blood flowed from it, and the sick person always recovered.

"Now if they really believed all of this, I wonder why they do not cut off the heads of all of the corpses as a means of security. I think if anyone was convinced of this wonderful infatuation, it would be easy to give credit to Witches, haunted houses and many other visible pranks of the Devil, which in modern times have gone out of fashion, except here at Notgrove and a few more such wild ignorant places that seem to be two hundred years behind the rest of the world in manners and wisdom.

"Hereabouts we have stone mountains of great weight, which walk about at night without help, even though several men can't budge them in the day time. There are white pots that will never bake, because they are bewitched, and other tales of similar enchantment. With both my brothers Jeff and Billy in Germany, it is natural that I should be concerned about them, and I am anxious to hear your opinion."

3

Guy Carleton, 1st Baron Dorchester (1724-1808)

In a time when both sexes married quite young, the governor of Quebec remained a bachelor until his forty-seventh year. One theory attributes his reluctance to a failed romance with a cousin when he was in his twenties. Another suggests that his income was insufficient to the prospect: aside from a £1,000 bequest from James Wolfe (under whom he served at the capture of Quebec) and a sum of prize money from a campaign in Cuba, Carleton was forced to live on his salary, a condition not always suitable for a gentleman. Yet on returning temporarily to England in 1770 he acted decisively in the matter of marriage. An old military friend, the second Earl of Effingham, had died a few years earlier, and Carleton dined in London with the new third Earl and his two younger sisters, Lady Anne and Lady Maria, nineteen and seventeen respectively, to all of whom he had long been an avuncular figure. Also present was a contemporary of the sisters, a Miss Seymour. After first retiring from the table and leaving the gentlemen to their port, the two sisters were summoned to return, whereupon Carleton proposed to Lady Ann. She refused and fled the room in tears (for she was in love with Carleton's nephew, whom she married subsequently). Lady Maria vouchsafed that she herself would not have rejected such a fine offer. A few weeks later, Miss Seymour contrived to pass along this intelligence to Carleton, who proposed and this time was accepted. Miss Seymour always took pride in her role as a matchmaker and perpetuated the story in the Dorchester family, where it persists to this day.

4

General James Wolfe (1727/28-59)

Wolfe was mortally wounded at the Plains of Abraham, as was his adversary Montcalm, but he lived long enough to comprehend his victory and then departed with style. One of his subordinates would later record the scene in his diary: "After our late worthy general, of renowed memory, was carried off wounded, to the rear of the front line, he desired those who were about him to lay him down; being asked if he would have a Surgeon, he replied, 'It is needless; it is all over with me.' One of them cried out, 'They run, see how they run.' 'Who runs?' demanded our hero, with great earnestness, like a person roused from sleep. The Officer answered, 'The enemy, Sir Egad they give way everywhere.' Thereupon the General rejoined, 'Go one of you, my lads, to Colonel Burton; tell him to march Webb's regiment with all speed down to Charles's river, to cut off the retreat of the fugitives from the bridge.' Then, turning on his side, he added, 'Now, God be praised, I will die in peace': and thus expired."

5
William Cobbett (1763-1835)

The great English radical, pamphleteer, and agrarian reformer, the author of *Cottage Economy, Rural Rides* and other famous works, started his career as a controversialist while serving six years in Nova Scotia and New Brunswick with the 54th Regiment of Foot. His stay began on a sad note. When the soldiers' baggage was brought ashore at Halifax, he lost a keepsake in the harbour: a copy of Swift's *A Tale of a Tub* that he had carried since boyhood. It was the first book he had ever owned, evidence of his voracious appetite for self-education which he continued to feed in the New World (it is typical of Cobbett that while on sentry duty he memorized in its entirety a work called *Lowth's Grammar*).

Soon he was regimental sergeant-major, charged with writing the official reports and dealing with paperwork generally. In that capacity, he was privy to the regiment's accounts. They gave him vivid proof of the corruption and misfeasance that he suspected were epidemic in the officer class, whose members' downward gaze he met with increased hatred. Cobbett left the army, marrying a Canadian, Ann Reid (who would carry on his work after his death). Then he promptly published a fiery attack on the British military, using figures he had been secreting for just such a purpose. The pamphlet was so fierce that he had to flee to the United States for a time to avoid imprisonment for libel (as later he would flee to England to sidestep similar difficulties in America). Thus was set in motion a long career of calumny, defiance, exile, and litigation.

6
Sir Alexander Mackenzie (1764-1820)

On neither of his famous expeditions—up the Mackenzie River to the Beaufort Sea in 1789 and from Lake Athabaska across the Rockies to the Pacific in 1793—did Mackenzie commit violence against the natives, though there were several tense moments. Nor did he lose a single member of either party. Perhaps his most remarkable trait as a leader was putting up with criticism in preference in putting down mutiny. His journals contain many reports of his men's caustic insolence and his own skilful adjuration.

When on the second voyage, for example, "it began to be muttered on all sides that there was no alternative but to return," he ordered camp be made on a high hill; carrying themselves and their equipment up the slope reduced the grumblers to silent exhaustion. Later, in order to lighten a canoe for a passage through some strong rapids, Mackenzie intended to lead a few of the occupants overland, "but those in the boat with great eagerness requested me to embark, declaring ... that, if they perished, I should perish with them." Perhaps because it was thus overloaded, the canoe was smashed up on some rocks and valuable supplies were lost. Again there was a chorus of negativism. "I listened ... to the observations that were made on the occasion without replying to them, till their panic was dispelled...."

The very next day one of the men flatly refused to continue the canoe journey. Mackenzie remarked: "I should not have passed it over without taking some very severe means to prevent a repetition of it; but as he had had the general character of a simple fellow, among his companions, and had been frightened out of what little sense he possessed, by our late dangers, I rather preferred to consider him as unworthy of accompanying us, and to represent him as an object of ridicule and contempt for his pusillanimous behaviour; though, in fact, he was a very useful, active, and laborious man."

When the men panicked in response to a slight Indian menace, Mackenzie proved effective once more. "Whatever might have been the wavering disposition of the people on former occasions, they were now decided in their opinions as to the necessity of returning without delay ... their cry was—'Let us reimbark, and be gone.' This, however, was not my design, and in a more peremptory tone than I usually employed, they were ordered to unload the canoe...."

He found his Indian guides to be equally troublesome. One of them was "manifesting continual signs of dissatisfaction [with] a service which he had found so irksome and full of danger." Others "began to complain of our mode of travelling, and mentioned their intention of leaving us ... and my interpreters ... were equally dissatisfied."

At length, many of the group resolved to desert, forgetting about canoes and river travel to strike out by themselves over the mountains. "I was all this time sitting patiently on a stone, and indulging the hope that, when their frantic terror had subsided, their returning reason would have disposed them to perceive the rashness of their project...." When it did not, he "proceeded to employ such arguments as I trusted would turn them from their senseless and impracticable purpose." He convinced them to remain, he reported, by means of simple mathematical logic.

7

William Lyon Mackenzie (1795-1861)

Few have appreciated Mackenzie's sanguine streak though it was obviously one component of what, viewed as a whole, can only be called his stubbornness. The trait was at its most obvious in 1849 when, eleven years after fleeing to avoid arrest for his part in the 1837 uprising, he ended his exile in the United States—only to find that emotions still ran strong back home.

"His arrival in Toronto", wrote Charles Lindsey, his son-in-law and first biographer, "was the signal for a Tory riot. On the evening of the 22d March, a mob collected in the streets, with flambeaux and effigies of Attorney General Baldwin, Solicitor General Blake, and Mackenzie. They marched defiantly past the Police Office, burnt two of the effigies opposite the residences of the Crown officers, and then proceeded up Yonge Street, to the house of Mr. John McIntosh, where Mr. Mackenzie was staying. Here, by the aid of two or three blazing tarbarrels, the mob burnt the remaining effigy and assailed the house, broke the windows, and attempted to force their way through the door. All the while, the Chief of Police and at least one member of the City Council were quietly looking on. Next day, the Mayor caused special constables to be sworn in with a view of preventing a repetition of these outrages; and an alderman, in his place in the Council, declared that he 'would not hesitate an instant' to assassinate Mackenzie, were he not restrained by fear of the law! For many nights after the house was well guarded, and was not again attacked. The *Examiner* condemned these outrages in fitting terms, and the premises of the proprietor were threatened with attack. A mob assembled in King Street for that purpose; but when it became known that there was a number of armed men in the building, they dispersed without attempting any violence. Two persons had been stationed on the ground floor with double-barrelled guns, and the first man who might have broken in would have been instantly shot."

Such a reception might have discouraged another type of personality. So great was Mackenzie's "confidence in his own popularity," however, "that he resolved to stand for the first constituency that might become vacant. It happened to be Haldimand: for which county he was elected in April, 1851, his principal opponent being Mr. George Brown."

8
Major John Richardson (1796-1852)

His birth in Queenston made Richardson, the author of *Wacousta* and many other works less well known, the first Canadian-born novelist. His thin skin and corresponding insensitivity to others made him a master duellist.

Shortly after the close of the Napoleonic Wars, Lieutenant Richardson, as he then was, challenged a fellow officer who had slighted the performing ability of a nineteen-year-old London actress known to Richardson only by reputation. They met in Hyde Park, and honour was satisfied when each man fired and missed the other. A few years later, in Paris, he challenged a notorious duellist, the Marquis du Hally, again for some remark reflecting ill on a woman. They met in the Bois de Boulogne with horse pistols, and Richardson was wounded in one ankle. In 1843, back in Canada where he edited first one newspaper and then another, Richardson fought a duel with a political rival in Kingston. Each antagonist fired once, to no effect, whereupon the seconds tried to resolve the matter without another volley. The result was disagreement about who had apologized to whom. After an hour, both groups departed in frustration.

9
Joseph Howe (1804-73)

If one of the great Nova Scotian's talents was an ability to provoke his political opponents, another was the way he could stop short of actually duelling. When a messenger brought a challenge from Sir Rupert George, the provincial secretary, Howe begged leave to decline the fight, saying that "never having had any personal quarrel with Sir Rupert, I should not fire at him" and that, in any event, he had "no great fancy for being shot by every public officer whose intellect I might happen to compare with his emoluments...." Such remarks had the desired effect in that his enemies "got laughed at and nobody blamed me." He conceded privately that "the honour was not equal to the risk...."

10
Sir George-Etienne Cartier (1814-73)

None of the other Fathers of Confederation had a more dramatic public life. He was one of the rebels of 1837. Ten years later he was standing for a seat in the Union parliament as a Reformer. Ten years after that he was co-premier, with John A. Macdonald, of the Province of Canada. And ten years after that, with Confederation a reality, he was in Sir John's cabinet. He was not without many accomplishments but was no stranger to intrigue. He was one of the moving spirits behind the Canadian Pacific Railway, for example, but likewise the author of the incriminating letter that brought down the government in the Pacific Scandal. He once attacked a law client with a cane and as late as 1848 he actually exchanged shots with a political opponent in a duel. He had an enormous appetite for politics, natural ability as an entrepreneur, and a perverse capacity for everything associated with English rather than Gallic culture. He was renowned for his love of food, music and entertaining. One of his guests recorded that "Mr. Cartier sang or croaked after dinner, and made every one he could find stand up, hold hands, and sing a chorus. The wretched servants brought in tea, and he pushed them away till after his song was over. He pushed one on his arm lightly, and I saw the servant rubbing his arm much annoyed, and looking like a dog with a trodden-on tail".

11
Sir John A. Macdonald (1815-91)

A substantial volume could be made of Sir John A. *anecdota*. This passage from the memoirs of Sir John Willison, the famous parliamentary correspondent and long-serving editor of the Toronto *Globe*, not only suggests what such a collection might be like but is itself notable for its flavour of authenticity.

"Sir John Macdonald was a man with his feet on the earth and his head not so far above it. He seldom sought to climb to moral elevations where the footing might be insecure. For a time he drank freely but any whisper of censure only stimulated Conservatives to fiercer personal loyalty. He said himself that the country would rather have 'John A.' drunk than George Brown sober. He warned D'Arcy McGee that 'this Government can't afford two drunkards and you've got to stop.' His drinking was exaggerated, as were his other faults and follies, by sleepless and insensate opponents. Very often the attack was so violent as to bring chivalrous souls to his side and actually react in his favour. Down to middle life and beyond Sir John Macdonald had periodical 'sprees' and nothing that he attempted was done badly. Sometimes he was disabled for public duty. The authorities seem to agree that not only may a 'spree' come unaware but that it is as uncertain in its going as in its coming. Begun in complete privacy it may develop various phases and attract more public notice than is desirable even though the performance may be original and artistic. Unlike any other pursuit every rehearsal is a performance and every presentation a surprise. The public seldom saw 'John A.' in liquor, but occasionally there were symptoms which even Conservatives could not mistake. Once he was to speak at a town on Lake Huron, but he was so long in sleeping off the consequences that the vessel on which he was a passenger dare not put into the harbour. That was fifty years ago but not yet have local Conservatives discovered any humour in the incident or become reconciled to the graceless chaffing of their Liberal neighbours. A common story, resting upon no adequate authority, is that a short-hand writer once undertook to make a verbatim report of a speech which Sir John delivered at Kingston. When he had examined the manuscript he sent for the reporter, gravely intimated that he had read portions of it with pain and surprise, and with the mild austerity of a grieving father added, 'Young man, if you ever again undertake to report the speech of a public man be sure that you keep sober.'

"There is an authenticated story of Macdonald in the early sixties. He was Attorney-General for Upper Canada, and lived in lodgings in Quebec. He had been absent from duty for a week; public business was delayed, and the Governor-General became impatient. He sent his aide-de-camp, young Lord Bury, to find the absent Minister. Pushing his way past the old house-keeper, Lord Bury penetrated to the bedroom where Macdonald was sitting in bed, reading a novel with a decanter of sherry on the table beside him. 'Mr. Macdonald, the Governor-General told me to say to you that if you don't sober up and get back to business, he will not be answerable for the consequences.' Macdonald's countenance reflected the anger he felt at the intrusion: 'Are you here in your official capacity, or as a private individual?' 'What difference does that make?' asked Lord Bury. 'Just this,' snapped the statesman, 'if you are here in your official capacity, you can go back to Sir Edmund Head, give him my compliments, and tell him to go to h---; if you are here simply as a private individual, you can go yourself.'"

12
George Brown (1818-80)

The co-founder of the Toronto *Globe,* an important moulding force
in the early years of the Liberal Party and one of the architects of
Confederation, was also active as a businessman, farmer, civic
leader, and philanthropist on many fronts simultaneously. He in fact
despised sloth as only a militant nineteenth-century Protestant could
do, but he also lamented one consequence of his busy-ness. A significant portion of his voluminous correspondence begins with profound
apologies for his tardiness in replying. So far behind was he in his
letter-writing that for much of his life he kept one "special pocket"
in his frock coat for letters of a more urgent personal nature than
the ones which filled the large box lodged permanently atop his desk.
Every so often he would empty the pocket and let its contents mingle
with those of the box. Then he would re-sort and re-prioritise the
whole mess once again. The habit was already well advanced when
Brown was in his thirties. It, and his habitual contrition, continued
the rest of his life.

13
Donald Smith, 1*st* Baron Strathcona (1820-1914)

On November seventh, 1885, Smith drove the Last Spike in the Canadian Pacific at Craigellachie in Eagle Pass, BC, thus connecting the
Atlantic to the Pacific by rail. On his first attempt with the sledge-
hammer, he succeeded only in bending a spike, which he later took
as a souvenir, along with the hammer. Neither it nor the one that
was quickly substituted was made of gold (the governor general had
ordered one made of silver but both he and it were unable to attend
the ceremony). There was nothing special about the last spike at
all, in fact. Sir William Van Horne said that anyone wishing to see
it in its place would have to pay full fare.

14
Sir Charles Tupper (1821-1915)

Tupper is now most commonly remembered for the length of his political career overall as contrasted with the shortness of his tenure as prime minister—a mere ten weeks. But his contemporaries naturally had a more complete impression of his character. One of them recalled "a thing which faithfully illustrates his temper and method." Looking at the shambles of Reciprocity and the fall of the Laurier government, Tupper "said the facts afforded final evidence that Laurier was neither a politician nor a statesman. If he had been a politician he would have dissolved Parliament and gone to the country as soon as the agreement was negotiated, while if he had been a statesman he never would have made the agreement. Whether or not Tupper would have made the agreement it is certain that he would have taken an immediate appeal to the constituents and probably have secured a favourable judgment before the Opposition could have adjusted itself to the situation." The writer continued: "It may be fair to soften this hard judgment upon Laurier for which I am not responsible with a hostile estimate of Tupper. Once when Sir Charles was speaking in Parliament with characteristic vigour and vehemence a Liberal member said to his deskmate, 'What a d--- liar that man Tupper is.' 'Yes,' was the reply, 'he just wastes lies.'"

15
Alexander Mackenzie (1822-92)

Canada's second prime minister was not the soul of tact. When a Tory accused him of not being loyal to the Crown, he replied, "Loyalty to the Queen does not require a man to bow down to her manservant, or her maidservant—or her ass." He told Benjamin

Disraeli that Canadians "were all but ruined from first to last by English diplomacy and treaty-making and we would have no more of it at any price." When he and his Liberals were turfed out, he wrote that the party must find a new leader who could meet his Conservative opposite number on equal footing, someone, that is, who had "graduated as a horse-thief or at least distinguished himself as having chiselled a municipality or robbed a railway company." His dying words were "Oh, take me home": a reference to Scotland or Heaven, it's not clear which.

16
Goldwin Smith (1823-1910)

Smith was the former Oxford don who presided over Canadian intellectual life in the last quarter of the nineteenth century and whose advocacy of union with the United States, as expressed in his infamous book *Canada and the Canadian Question* (1891), won him well-earned opprobrium.

"In his memoirs Goldwin Smith speaks with extreme contempt for the whole social circle which surrounded him during his long residence in Toronto", Hector Charlesworth wrote. "And when I think of how people used to mention his views and utterances almost with bated breath, and thrust him into the limelight of every public occasion as 'Exhibit A' to prove the city's distinction and culture, his words savour of ingratitude.

"Arnold Haultain, for many years his secretary and later his biographer, more than hints that in Goldwin Smith's incessant though at times covert support of the annexation movement, he cherished the dream that if it were ever accomplished the people of this continent would be so grateful that they would elect him President, — which shows how far out of touch with realities even the finest minds may become...

"It is sad to have to say it, but Goldwin Smith was a much more

vitriolic writer under cover of anonymity than in his signed articles…
Going through the Morgan collection of manuscripts in the New York
Public Library recently I saw a manuscript, 'Berlin and Afghanistan,'
by Goldwin Smith, the collector's value of which lies in the fact that
it never succeeded in finding a publisher. It was locked up in a glass
case, and I could not help wondering what it contained that it should
have been suppressed.

"Goldwin Smith dealt rather a harsh blow to the city in which he
resided so long, and to the University whose staff had always
delighted to honour him, when he left a large fortune to Cornell
University at Ithaca, N.Y., where he had been for a brief period
professor of history, many years before. The injustice of the gift
was emphasized by the fact that Cornell was in no need of en-
dowments, whereas University College has always been in straitened
circumstances. A fair division at least would have been acceptable.
After his wife's death Goldwin Smith grew more discontented with
Toronto than ever, and announced his intention of ending his days
at Ithaca. An accident followed by a lingering illness prevented his
carrying out this intention. A Scottish newspaper friend of mine made
a very shrewd comment on the bequest to Cornell, when he said:
'It's hard luck that Goldwin Smith did not go to live at Cornell University. In three months time he would have become so sore at not
receiving enough attention that he would have changed his will in
favour of the University of Toronto.' Beyond a doubt that is what
would have happened. Discontent with his surroundings was a rul-
ing phase of his temperament. In his Oxford days he had but little
praise for that University; yet as a voluntary exile in Canada, he
wrote of it in phrases of haunting beauty."

17
Amor De Cosmos (1825-97)

De Cosmos, formerly William Alexander Smith, helped to lead British Columbia into Confederation and from 1872 to 1874 was both its premier and a federal MP. Once his political career reached its conclusion, however, he became extremely eccentric. It was said that he used boot blacking on his beard as well as his footwear, for example. And although Victoria could boast of electrified tramcars by the early 1890s, De Cosmos would not patronise them, as he was afraid of electricity. He walked everywhere instead, carrying a cane or brolly as a weapon, although on one occasion the practice seems to have done him no good. At a chance meeting in the street, he "applied opprobrious epithets" and later his fist to a local coal baron, who "retaliated by wearing out an umbrella on his assailant's head and shoulders." Indeed it was clear that his eccentricity was deteriorating into serious mental illness. In 1895 he decided to stand for Parliament once again but his name was withdrawn after he rose to speak at a rally and found himself at a complete loss for words of any sort. He was later declared mad.

18
John H.R. Molson (1826-97)

As this Molson (one of the grandchildren of the founder of the dynasty) lay dying, he dictated a message to his descendants, those already born and those yet to come.

"The Molson Family", he began, "has maintained and preserved its position and influence by steady, patient industry, and every member should be a real worker and not rely upon what it has been.

All that is good and great of the family should not be underground.

"Your private life should be pure. Make no compromise with vice, be able to say no in a firm manly manner.

"Character is the real test of manhood. Live within your income no matter how small it may be. Permanent wealth is maintained and preserved by vigilance and prudence and not by speculation.

"Be just, and generous when you have the means.

"Wealth will not take care of itself if not vigilantly cared for..."

Molson died before he could complete the document.

He left instructions that his body be cremated. The procedure was so rarely practised at the time that Canada did not possess a single crematorium, and the deed had to be performed in Boston. His ashes were returned to Canada and interred in the family plot in a Montreal cemetery. But somehow the rumour spread that his widow was keeping the ashes in a black lacquered box at home. "This erroneous belief caused any child who peeked into the study to feel a shiver of fear", the family historian has written. Had such visitors dared to open the lid, however, they would have learned that the object in question was a music box.

19

Sir Sandford Fleming (1827-1915)

Sir Sandford was a man of many accomplishments: the foremost Canadian engineer of his day and the creator of standard time and the present system of time-zones used throughout the world. He also designed the first Canadian postage stamp, and it is this last achievement that seems unusual, given that he suffered from colour blindness. "As a young man paying court to his future wife, he one day chose what seemed to him a fine piece of cloth and had his tailor in Toronto make him a suit from it", a contemporary wrote. "This he donned and started for an Easter visit to the distant home of his fiancée. He was charmed with the merry parties he encountered all the way on the train to Prescott and thence on the stage to his destination, but was unconscious of the cause of amusement until the young lady answered his knock at the door, when she screamed with hilarity at the sight of his suit. It was a bright pink! She chose his suits and neckties after that."

20
Edward Blake (1833-1912)

The nineteenth-century Liberal leader has been called the greatest Canadian statesman never to have been prime minister. Indeed the career of this complex, mercurial, repressed, and socially awkward politician is a useful foil to the modern notion that it is only in the television age that personality and image have determined success in public life. Blake, who was Ontario premier for a brief period before devoting himself to federal politics, was renowned for his joyless brand of morality (his one secret vice was photographing all the rooms of his house). His lack of friends arose partly from his legalistic debating style, which one contemporary parodied with deadly accuracy: "If you believe me, what need is there for explanations? ... and if you do not believe me you stand condemned." He was for many years the bitter rival of Sir John A. Macdonald. But even when he was the winner on moral grounds, as he was in regard to ethical questions surrounding the Canadian Pacific Railway, he was no match for Sir John's Bacchic charm and ready compromise. One observer referred to "His paw, chilly as the fin of a dead fish" when he shook hands. Another saw him at a banquet and reported, "I looked at his shirtfront and then at his face, and concluded that it didn't matter which I looked at as they were both starched and ironed."

21
Timothy Eaton (1834-1907)

The founder of the famous department stores that bear his name was a shy and taciturn figure, but could become quite voluble "when you touched the chords of his philosophy", according to J.W.L. Forster, the Canadian portrait painter. "I once remarked upon the cost of living and wage levels as leaving little margin between", Forster recalled. "That seemed to awaken him. 'I've worked overtime for forty years and it hasn't hurt me', he said. 'If a man really wants to get ahead, is there any better way? Tell me that!' 'A man who works longer hours than meets his needs will have a margin of profit; that gives his family comforts and he and the whole country prosper. How else will it be done? Tell me.'

"'Another thing, Mr. Forster: If a good workman can live on what he earns in three days and he won't work four, he loses self-respect, and raises the cost of everything. How will you keep costs down unless everyone keeps faith with himself and with others? Tell me that.

"'And tell me, who does a man work for if not himself? Does he not use a manager's brains to supply him with something to do, that gives him a living? He's got a job, and the good spirit he shows in his work makes his work good, and that betters his chances, for he's working for himself, isn't he? Isn't that true?' The honest light of his eye and the play of his features showed how sincere he was in his questions."

22

Dr Richard Maurice Bucke (1837-1902)

As a young man, the pioneer Canadian psychiatrist, who was also the friend, executor and authorized biographer of Walt Whitman, took part in the discovery of the great Nevada silver fields. "He met and became friends with the Grosh brothers and their partner Brown, who had discovered the vast deposits of silver known later as the Comstock Lode but were keeping their find dark while they prospected ever further for more silver. Disaster overtook them—Brown and one of the Groshes died, and the other brother, Allan, with Bucke set out over the mountains, although it was winter, in an attempt to reach the Coast. It was a terrible experience—Allan Grosh died on the way, and Bucke with both feet frozen was rescued at the last minute by a mining party. The result was that Bucke had to have the whole of one foot and part of the other amputated, and that after a whole winter in bed, he returned to life a young man of 21 so badly maimed that for the 40 years remaining to him he was never free from pain for more than a few hours at a time."

In 1872, after spending an evening with friends reading poetry, Dr Bucke experienced what he called his Illumination.

"All at once, without warning of any kind," he wrote later, using the third person instead of the first, "he found himself wrapped around, as it were, by a flame-colored cloud. For an instant he thought of fire—some sudden conflagration in the great city. The next he knew that the light was within himself.

"Directly after there came upon him a sense of exultation, of immense joyousness, accompanied or immediately followed by an intellectual illumination quite impossible to describe. Into his brain streamed one momentary lightning-flash of the Brahmic Splendor which ever since lightened his life. Upon his heart fell one drop of the Brahmic Bliss, leaving thenceforward for always an aftertaste of Heaven."

Thus the beginning of his interest in untapped psychic energy, a concern that led to his famous book *Cosmic Consciousness,* published in 1901.

23
James J. Hill (1838-1916)

Hill was one of the original directors of the Canadian Pacific and later became a railway baron in the US as well. In his diary, the French art dealer René Gimpel, who helped many robber barons of the period to build important collections of paintings, repeats a story about him.

"He was a dock worker somewhere in Canada, and used to have lunch and dinner at a restaurant with about twenty-five other dock workers, all thrifty and all sparing in their tips to the waitress; but on Christmas Eve Hill got up and asked them all if they were prepared to give the girl the same sum as he. They said yes, particularly as they knew Hill was even stingier than they. He put $20 on the table. They were horrified, but they were men of honor: they had given their word, and they kept it.

"Twelve days later Hill married the waitress."

24
Kootenai Brown (1839-1916)

At one time or another, Brown, whose nickname derived from his travels in the area of the Kootenay gold rush in British Columbia, followed many of the glamorous frontier professions. He was, for example, a constable, a prospector, a soldier, a whisky trader, a buffalo hunter and a scout (and towards the end of his life became a conservationist of note). One of his most colourful exploits took place in 1869 when he worked across the border in the Dakota Territory, for a private company that carried the mail for the US military.

He and a companion "were within half a mile of Strawberry Lake," he recalled, "and it was about seven o'clock in the evening of the twenty-fourth of May, the Queen's birthday. I have good reason to remember the date. We jumped off our horses and crept to the top of the hill to take a good look for Indians... Getting on our horses again we rode down to cross this coulee and to get to the camping grounds by the lake. Just as we went down the steep bank the Indians charged on us yelling out 'Don't shoot, don't be fools, we're friends....'

"In the dash they made at us Sitting Bull was leading, riding a fine big grey horse... In the melee that followed, Lady Jane Grey, our pack mule, broke away and started for Fort Stevenson as fast as she could travel, but the Sioux took after her, soon captured her and appropriated everything in our pack....

"Sitting Bull ordered us to get off our horses and when we did he had us stripped as naked as the day we were born. They took everything, despatches, mail, guns, horses, clothes.... Some of the young bucks began yelling 'Kash-ga, Kash-ga', meaning kill them, kill them. Sitting Bull raised his hand and shouted, 'Don't be in a hurry, we'll make a fire and have some fun with them.' We understood every word they said, of course, and we knew that Sitting Bull meant some playful mode of torture that the Sioux often inflicted on their captives."

Before that could happen, Brown's partner pleaded with Sitting Bull to be spared on the grounds that he was part Santee Sioux, as indeed he was. But he then stretched Sitting Bull's credulity by making the same claim for Brown. The great chief was skeptical, acknowledging that Brown spoke the language well but observing that "your skin is very white and your eyes are blue." Brown contended that he and his friend had simply been passing southwards from the prairies when the American soldiers pressed on them "some letters to carry for one trip".

In the meantime a dispute arose concerning division of the prisoners' property, and a council was called to settle the matter. By then it was dark and the two mail-carriers escaped by rolling a hundred feet down the coulee and into the lake, where they hid in the weeds in water up to their necks while their captors searched madly, firing at random. "It was blowing a regular hurricane and pouring down torrents of rain and this is probably what saved us," Brown would write.

Once it was clear that the Sioux had gone off to search for them elsewhere, the two men slipped away in the direction of Fort Stevenson, fighting the effects of exposure, hunger and, when the sun came up, mosquitos.

"Our travel was slow during the night but when daylight came and we got our bearings we made good time... There was bastions in the Fort and one of the sentries saw us coming. He reported to the Sergeant of the guard, and he in turn reported to the officer of the day that two Indians were approaching the Fort bare naked. The guard was sent out to capture us but when the Sergeant saw who we were he ran to meet us with 'what's up? what's up?' I replied, 'Oh, nothing much. The Sioux have your mail, horses, and our clothes, and came very near getting us. We have walked from Strawberry Lake."

25

Sir Wilfrid Laurier (1841-1919)

When he became leader of the Liberals in 1887, Laurier surprised many observers by the assertiveness and energy he showed in rebuilding the party nationally. He took them unawares because throughout his already long public life he had seemed so bookish, retiring, and undemonstrative. The journalist John (later Sir John) Willison had once overheard Laurier and Goldwin Smith in learned conversation about collecting rare cookbooks. He was therefore startled by an incident that took place during an address Laurier delivered in Cannington, Ontario. "An Anglican clergyman with gross discourtesy arose in the meeting and shouted that they could not learn the true way from a Roman Catholic. Laurier retorted with passionate energy, 'You could—in politics', and he proceeded in sentences of stern rebuke to flog the interrupter into humiliation and silence. The rest of the speech was animated and confident...." The outburst was a foretaste of what would follow in the years ahead.

"It is curious that the qualities of decision and resolution which Laurier possessed in such remarkable degree were those in which he was thought deficient", Willison went on. "It is just as remarkable that despite his reputation for indolence when he became Prime Minister he was an example of industry in office, indefatigable in his attendance in Parliament and diligent and vigorous in the direction of the party which he recreated and over which he exercised such complete authority. No one who had knowledge of his career in Quebec before he became a national figure could have doubted his courage, but his comparative inaction in Parliament from 1878 to 1887 explains many misconceptions which prevailed in the other Provinces."

26

Oronhyatekha (1841-1907)

Oronhyatekha was a Mohawk from near Brantford, Ontario, who became a famous physician and the worldwide head of the Independent Order of Foresters, a fraternal organisation which he used to build a large and profitable insurance company. The turning point in his life came in 1860 when he was introduced to the Prince of Wales, later Edward VII, who was visiting a Six Nations reserve as part of his Canadian tour. Learning that the young man had already begun to put himself through a small college in the United States,

Sir Henry Acland, a member of the Prince's entourage, expressed the hope that he would carry on with his education. He added, "One day we may expect to see you at Oxford." Oronhyatekha misread or ignored the facetious nature of the remark and promptly turned up in England on Sir Henry's academic doorstep. As it happened, he left Oxford after three years for the University of Toronto, becoming the first native person to win a medical degree at a Canadian institution.

James Mavor, the economist, visited him at his house in the 1890s and found him an indiscriminate collector of objects and an egotist. "He had a replica of the Coronation Chair, upholstered in velvet and lavishly decorated with gold ... extraordinary pictures on the walls ... the most dreadful of modern vases in marble and bronze ... and dominating everything, a life-sized statue of Oronhyatekha himself in plaster painted to look life like." Mavor also witnessed a family feast and thus got to know Oronhyatekha the gourmand. "To say that the table was loaded with viands would convey no accurate idea. It was loaded and emptied and loaded again. Geese were brought and consumed, and more geese were brought and consumed until a fair-sized flock had been sacrificed. Oronhyatekha explained to me that an Indian must eat until he can eat no longer, and that this was a surviving trait of his nomadic and uncertain life." Mavor apparently believed him.

27
David Boyle (1842-1911)

In addition to being the father of Canadian archaeology, particularly Central Canadian archaeology, and the curator of what became the Royal Ontario Museum, Boyle was highly regarded internationally as well, for he was among those who took the field out of the hands of scavengers and made it a respectable branch of scientific inquiry. Two other sides of his character may be observed in the fact that he wrote nationalistic doggerel for children and took violent exception to the manner in which it was reviewed. The book in question was *Uncle Jim's Canadian Nursery Rhymes for Family and Kindergarten Use*, illustrated by C.W. Jeffreys and published in 1908. The operative word was Canadian. Like Dennis Lee some sixty years later, he was offended by the dependence on Old World references in Mother Goose and sought to supply an all-Canadian alternative. His subjects included beavers, maple leaves and the Canadian Pacific Railway. Alas, his versecraft, most notably his sense of rhythm, was deplorable.

Tommy Temper had a fall
He bumped his brow and gave a bawl;
As soon's his head had struck the floor,
Niagara never gave such a roar.

The book appeared anonymously, and Boyle was furious when a commentator in *The Canadian Magazine* broke his cover. He wrote: "If you knew how taring, rearing, ripping, ranting mad I was when I saw that you mentioned my name in connection with the work, you would avoid me as you value your life, if we were to face one and other [*sic*] in a ten acre field."

28
Sir William Van Horne (1843-1915)

Roger Fry, the seminal English art critic and one of the strongest intellectual forces in the Bloomsbury group, had occasion to know many North American establishment figures during his term as curator of the Metropolitan Museum of Art in New York. When the builder of the Canadian Pacific Railway passed away, leaving a Montreal mansion rich with valuable and sometimes important paintings, Fry was able to draw on personal recollection for an obituary in *The Burlington Magazine* of London. He learned to his chagrin, however, that the gulf between North American and British usage had grown wide. He was later obliged to apologize to Sir William's family for stating that he had drunk beer with the great man in a "saloon", which he believed approximated what the English call a saloon bar. He also regretted having said that the magnate's language was "racy" at times. "Here it is always used as praise", Fry backpedalled. "No one would suppose that it even denoted the freedom of speech employed in Shakespeare or the Bible."

29
Louis Riel (1844-85)

The editor and broadcaster Hector Charlesworth recalling Victoria MacVicar, a western pioneer who was his grandfather's first cousin:
"She came into especial prominence in connection with Louis Riel's first rising in 1870. The picture she gave us of Riel was quite different from the villainous conception we all had of him in the East after his second rising in 1885, for which he was tried and hanged. They had been boy and girl together, and at one time Riel was in love with her. She spoke of him as a dreamy, handsome, clever youth, half mad with ambition. I think history bears out this view... At any rate, MacVicar had a great deal of influence over Riel; and when he started his rebellion in 1870 she was sent for to come from Fort William and see what she could do with him. She found that he had imprisoned a large number of white residents of Fort Garry and was threatening them with death as a reprisal for the accidental killing of a crazy follower of his. After several interviews she did finally induce Riel to release all but Thomas Scott, whom to his own misfortune, he ordered to be shot. It was memory of the murder of Scott that closed the door to a reprieve for him in 1885 after his second rising, when Blake, Laurier, and other prominent statesmen of the East were demanding it...."

"Victoria MacVicar told us that after the release had been arranged, Riel said, 'Victoria, I want you to stay and breakfast with me.' Whereat she rushed from the room with the words, 'I will never break bread with a rebel.' If true it seems to me a tasteless and indiscreet outburst, though characteristically feminine. But Riel was gentleman enough to keep his word, and she honoured him for that. Probably he knew that she was an intense loyalist who from childhood had taken very seriously the fact that she was named after Princess Victoria, while the latter was heiress apparent.

"Victoria MacVicar's visits to us were frequent during the whole period of the second Riel affair, which with the trial and subsequent agitation lasted long. It troubled her that this friend of childhood was to be hanged. She was an ardent spiritualist, like so many persons who have lived in the wilds, and related a singular story of psychic occurrences on the occasion in the autumn of 1885 when he was executed in Regina. She was at that time visiting Chicago, and early on the morning of the fatal day visited a medium to learn whether he was really to hang or whether a reprieve had arrived at the last moment. While the interview was in progress, she avowed that the face of the medium, who had gone into a trance as part of the usual ritual, changed horribly. Then she heard a sound like the pulling of a bolt, and the medium said, 'Your friend has passed into the beyond.' But she did not get a message from Riel, which I assume was what she sought. My mother warned us children that this was all nonsense, the work of Victoria's too vivid imagination. But it was blood-curdling to hear her relate it with absolute conviction."

30
Sir John Thompson (1844-94)

Canada's fourth prime minister—who, according to Sir John A. Macdonald, was "a little too fond of satire, and a little too much of a Nova Scotian"—was the father of the federal Criminal Code and a person of sound instincts. "These Yankee politicians", he once observed, "are the lowest race of thieves in existence". He died during a luncheon with Queen Victoria at Windsor Castle, an hour or so after being sworn in as member of the Privy Council.

31
Brother André (1845-1937)

Brother André was the name-in-religion of Alfred Bessette who founded St Joseph's Oratory in Montreal. His powers as a faith healer made him Quebec's most popular and in some ways most influential religious figure, particularly amongst the working class. Fellow members of the Congregation of the Holy Cross, and of other orders with which he came into contact, were sometimes moved to marvel at the severity of his diet. When he was the porter at the College of Notre-Dame-du-Sacré-Coeur in Côtes-des-Neiges, he fell to dining alone (a custom the bureaucrats in Rome thought showed lack of communal spirit). Except on those days when he fasted, his meals consisted of a little bread soaked in watered-down milk—and plenty of black coffee. In time, even the thought of any remotely normal diet became indigestible, though he dared not say so for "it might hurt the cook's feelings". During the serious illnesses that punctuated his life, he asked for, and would accept, nothing but wheat flour in hot salted water. "But is it glue that you wish?" asked a nursing sister, disbelievingly. "Yes, it is glue", he answered. In his final days, a nurse tried to substitute corn starch for the wheat flour but couldn't fool the patient. "After that I made the flour gruel six or seven times following Brother André's instructions", she remembered. "And strangely, this stuff I called paste, this unappetizing melange, Brother André appeared to enjoy and his stomach retained it."

32
Alexander Graham Bell (1847-1922)

"The story of my visit to Beinn Bhreagh [Bell's home on Cape Breton] is one with a joke on me", recalled the artist J.W.L. Forster. "I went thither to paint a portrait of Dr. Bell for a private collection. The portrait was painted in left profile, with Dr. Bell wearing a brown velvet smoker. When it was completed and I was packing to leave, Mr. Gilbert Grosvenor, one of his sons-in-law, came merrily into the room, exclaiming, 'Forster, you've done what no one of my knowledge has accomplished for nineteen years; you've brought unity into this family.' I asked the joke. He answered: 'They're all agreed the portrait is perfect, and they're all agreed that you shan't have it.' I protested, but asked, 'How about Dr. Bell giving sittings for another portrait?' 'Oh, he'll be delighted to give sittings, he's having the time of his life.' The first portrait went to the National Geographic Society's home in Washington, founded by Dr. Graham Bell.

"Time was required to paint the second, which I designed in larger style, Dr. Bell in grey worsted Norfolk and knickers and showing a three-quarter view. This one I did not get, because Mrs. Bell, who had taken special interest in its production, claimed it; and so I had to start all over again with another new portrait scheme. This time I painted Dr. Bell's majestic head in full view, with his figure in plum velvet smoker.

When the third was finished, special compliments were paid to it, which were appreciated sincerely as I went about packing up my picture. Dr. Bell, however, made the situation clear by saying, 'It's no idle compliment, Mr. Forster; the portrait is wanted for the Volta Bureau in Washington.' I had gone to paint a picture for myself; I painted three, and didn't get any of them. That was the joke on me. Later, at his Washington home, I painted a fourth portrait in academic gown and hood, which I have been able to retain, of the man whose memory we wake every time we use a telephone."

33
William Cruikshank (1848-1922)

The Canadian artist was related to George Cruikshank, the English illustrator associated with Dickens.

"'Cruik', as he was known to the fraternity, was a black, beetle-browed, bearded Scot, and a great draughtsman, who in New York before coming to Canada had taught Charles Dana Gibson to draw. He was a recluse who, as it was said, seemed to live on the smell of an oil rag. Yet when he died it was found that he had accumulated over $20,000, safely invested, though he had worked very little and had mainly subsisted on his salary as a teacher, than whom there was none better. 'Cruik' was a discerning critic of the works of other men and his views were highly valued by them; and his own pictures were thoroughly national...

"Homer Watson's home at Doon in the heart of the beautiful pastoral country of Western Ontario has for many years been a meeting place for artists. One summer Cruikshank and the brilliant landscape painter Carl Ahrens were Watson's guests, and on a fine day were proceeding along a country road and arguing about art. The eyes of the three were fascinated by the sight of a farmer plowing in a perfect setting for a picture. 'Cruik' began to rhapsodize in this wise: 'Look at yon man! He is a man of sense! He is not worrying about art! He is thinking of his land, and of the harvest he will reap. He is a useful man, – the true citizen.' The farmer just then reached the end of his furrow and waited to talk to the pedestrians. As they came up he said in German accents: 'Say, wouldn't it be fine if Doon could get a prass pand?' 'Cruik' walked on in a brown study and after several moments ejaculated mournfully: 'Yon man was a damn fool after all!'"

34

HRH Princess Louise, Duchess of Argyle (1848-1939)

"I vividly recall the furore over the coming of the Princess Louise [a daughter of Queen Victoria] as consort of the Marquis of Lorne, afterwards Duke of Argyle, when he became Governor General in 1878", wrote Hector Charlesworth. "My mother and aunts were openly disappointed because she was not more beautiful – for, never having seen a princess, they had apparently cherished a theory that beauty was part of the inheritance of such an exalted being."

35

Sir Edmund Walker (1848-1924)

The Rev J.A. Macdonald, the editor of the Toronto *Globe,* "could usually conduct the conversation for any group in which he was associated, and was apt to regard others who expressed opinions in his presence as over-talkative." Thus when someone mentioned Sir Edmund Walker, the chairman of the Canadian Bank of Commerce, he replied, "Oh, Sir Edmund's all right, but he has too much to say. I walked down St. George Street with him the other morning and I couldn't get a word in edgewise." A couple of days later, the person to whom the remark was addressed chanced to mention Macdonald in a meeting with Sir Edmund and "could hardly refrain from laughter when the banker said: 'Macdonald means well, but he's a very tedious man. I walked down St. George Street with him the other morning and I couldn't get a word in edgewise.'"

36
Sir William Osler (1849-1919)

One day Dr Osler's young niece met him as he left the home of a patient.

"Is she very ill?" the child asked.

"Very ill", he replied. "I fear she is apt to die."

The girl was saddened—and startled when, in a moment or two, her uncle began to whistle. She asked him why, and he answered, "I whistle that I may not weep."

It was perhaps from similar motivation that the physician and McGill University professor, the most famous medical person in the English-speaking world even before accepting the Regius chair of medicine at Oxford, so often engaged in practical jokes and pranks.

The impulse found expression in his creation of Egerton Y. Davis. This was more than a pseudonym, it was a rival personality. Not only would Osler adopt the name to ward off unwanted visitors and correspondents, but he once used it to submit a spurious article to the *Canadian Medical and Surgical Journal*; the paper concerned the supposed obstetrical practices of West Coast Indians.

One of his biographers has postulated that it must have been Davis and not Osler who, in an address at Johns Hopkins University in the US, argued facetiously that people should be put to death at age sixty: a remark that the press took seriously, with scandalous results.

37
Sir Sam Hughes (1853-1921)

"There was much that was romantic in the personality of Sir Sam", the flamboyant politician and soldier who had to be relieved of his military duties during the South African War and again during the First World War. "His temperament was that of the cut and thrust heroes of the Napoleonic wars, and despite his vitality I doubt if any man who held responsibilities at the outbreak [of the Great War] lived more exclusively in the past. One of his rooted convictions was that the war would be won by the bayonet, and his laudation of an invention by a woman secretary, consisting of a combined spade and shield which could be used for trench digging and then fitted over the barrel of the rifle to protect the soldier as he advanced to the charge, aroused a good deal of legitimate satire."

38
Frank Oliver (1853-1933)

The Alberta journalist-turned-politician, "who had carried his little newspaper press across the prairie in an ox-cart and had patiently published the Edmonton *Bulletin* under formidable frontier difficulties, was still an Independent with a seat far back among the Liberals. True, he became progressively less Independent and at the end of the process was appointed [Sir Wilfrid Laurier's] Minister of the Interior... He had the gift of tongues, one of which was suitable for polite conversation and the other was not. His parliamentary speeches were delivered with extraordinary intensity and suggested an outboard motor addicted to backfiring. One of the pastimes of the more light-hearted legislators in those days was to send a note to this speaker or to that in the hope of interrupting his train of thought. An innocent little page boy took one of these missives to the Honourable Frank in the midst of one of his staccato performances. He knew the game. His speech went on unbroken, except for the inclusion of one word: 'Getthehelloutofhere.'"

39
Sir Robert Borden (1854-1937)

The journalist Augustus Bridle on Canada's eighth prime minister:

"So he goes with that Derby hat and thick overcoat, trudging a bit sidewise up Parliament Hill on winter days to the office of the Premier in the East Block—the man who never laughs in public. Step by step he cogitates. Resolutely he holds on his way. Courteously he bows to a member or a minister. On into his room, face chiselled like bronze for an Egyptian god, grey hair punctiliously parted amidships, faultlessly groomed, a thick grizzled moustache, and a steady eye—always seeming to have plenty of time, forever seeming to make up his mind, discreetly shuffling over papers, reflectively reading; such a serious, meditative man. His secretary is staccato; Borden—always slowly polite and for the most part gently reasonable. In an hour he may conscientiously get through a load of detail work and is ready for the first of a line of miscellaneous callers....

"Sir Robert Borden never rises above the level of his work, because his work always seems to him the greatest thing in life. Personal ambition he never had, or if he had he kept it concealed with consummate actorship of which no one suspects him. Chicanery he never understood. He is a moral figure who sometimes finds himself at the mercy of a flippant, adventurous world. Conscious of certain limitations he has tried to overcome them. Once a photographer, anxious to get realistic action pictures of Mr. Borden during the campaign of 1907, enticed him on to the roof of a Toronto hotel where he had the Opposition leader enact a series of oratorical poses which were published by party organs as genuine pictures of Mr. Borden speaking. That is about the limit of Sir Robert Borden's guile."

40
James Mavor (1854-1925)

The great political economist (whose descendants, such as Dora Mavor Moore, Mavor Moore and others, have tended to be important in the performing arts) always would remember a *faux pas* he committed shortly after his arrival from Britain. He was given an audience by Sir Oliver Mowat, the Ontario premier, and several members of his cabinet. Sir Oliver asked what progress was being made in the fight for Home Rule for Scotland.

"None at all", Mavor told him.

"Why?"

"Because everyone knows that if there were Home Rule in Scotland the government of the country would fall into the hands of a few Edinburgh lawyers."

"Would that be a bad thing?" the premier wanted to know.

"The rest of the country apparently thinks so", Mavor told him.

"I then realised that Sir Oliver was himself a lawyer, and that nearly all his Cabinet were lawyers also."

41
Dr Augusta Stowe Gullen (1855-1933)

Gullen became famous as the first woman in Canada to practise medicine legally, though she was not the first Canadian woman trained to do so. Her mother, Emily Stowe (a founder of what became the Canadian Women's Suffrage Association, which her daughter would later head) had been refused a place in medical school in Canada and only barely had gained admittance to a New York one, graduating in 1869. But she was not able to establish a practice in either country.

Most of the same obstacles confronted her daughter a generation later, but she was able finally to win a place at Victoria College in Cobourg, Ontario, though had to endure daily taunts and prejudice from students and faculty. The pressure became unbearable, and one day she exploded in the classroom. "Surely you've had enough fun out of my being here", she said. "Surely you can see that all I want to do is to learn about medicine without disturbing anybody—just to do my work quietly. I don't interfere with you, or bother you. Don't you think the time has come to get some other form of entertainment? For sweet pity's sake, won't you let me be?" A long silence ensured. It was broken only when the instructor asked, "Can the class begin, young lady?"

She graduated in 1883 just as the situation was improving, for she immediately began teaching at the Women's Medical College which had been created earlier in the year. In 1909 she was one of the founders of Women's College Hospital, Toronto. When a visitor noted the all-female staff, from orderlies to administrators, and asked whether everyone in the hospital was female, the reply was, "Of course not. Half the babies born are male."

When a friend reported overhearing some disparaging remarks about her speech and appearance, Gullen was philosophical. "Tell the woman I heartily agree with her", she said. "I never like the way I speak. I have never liked the way I dress, although I have had one or two good frocks in my time; and my looks have been a constant source of distress to me all my life."

42
Sir Herbert Holt (1856-1941)

In an age of unbridled capitalism, Sir Herbert's was even less bridled than most. He enjoyed a monopoly on hydroelectric power in Montreal and was president of the Royal Bank. Those facts, however, scarcely begin to show the extent of his influence. "We get up in the morning and switch on Holt's lights," a Montrealer complained in the 1920s, "cook breakfast on Holt's gas, smoke one of Holt's cigarettes, read the morning news printed on Holt's paper, ride to work on one of Holt's streetcars, sit in an office heated by Holt's coal, then at night go to a film in one of Holt's theatres." He was arguably Canada's most hated businessman, and reasonably so, though it is not always possible to distinguish cause from effect. He was threatened frequently, and one shareholder even went so far as to shoot him. On another occasion he knocked two CPR employees unconscious (they too had been trying to murder him). In the Mount Royal Club he once leaned across the table and struck his bridge partner in the jaw. When a newspaper reporter called on him for details of one of his misunderstandings, Sir Herbert, ever the soul of tact, personally threw him down the stairs.

His fellow businessmen, such as Lord Atholstan, the publisher of the Montreal *Star,* liked him no better, as witness a story from the middle 1930s. It was always Atholstan's policy to publish the names of all those who contributed to what later became the United Way. Only his own contributions were to be kept anonymous. But one year he chanced to ask the canvasser how much Sir Herbert had given. When told the amount was $15,000, he pledged ten times as much and duly printed "Lord Atholstan, $150,000" in the *Star.* By such a tactic did he arouse what little sense of shame his nemesis may have possessed, and for appearances' sake Sir Herbert Holt had to dip into his pockets again.

Sir John Willison (1856-1927)

Willison abandoned the editorship of the Toronto *Globe* in 1902 in order to pursue "independent" journalism with a new paper, the *News*. In so doing he dealt a serious blow to the system under which newspapers were mere instruments of the various political parties. For decades he was also the Canadian correspondent of *The Times* of London. No subsequent Canadian newspaper editor has enjoyed quite the same level of power and respect. Among his proudest possessions, however, was "a beautiful collection of anonymous letters", often threatening in character, which he accumulated over the years. He recorded his "genuine delight in rereading their curious messages. I find an old envelope addressed to 'J.S. Willison, proprietor of Cox and Jaffray's morals and daylight editor of *The Globe*'. A letter which preserves the balance reads, 'The daily shift of the knightly editor defending Rogers is enough to make angels weep.' Another letter reads, 'You can beat Ananias; better not yell political purity so long as you have stinking fish in your own basket.' Of like implication was a letter I received four or five years ago, just a few minutes before I had to address the Canadian Club in Vancouver, 'You are the biggest liar in Canada. It is a wonder you were not shot long ago.' At least there is comfort in the reflection that one is not an amateur. Another of which I have lost the connection but which is signed 'A Conservative' reads, 'It must be something of a wrench to have to do this sort of thing, so long as one retains any pretensions to decency in public affairs. Surely the Prussian taskmaster could not be harder than this indicates. I take it that there was no escape, or you would have ignored the rascal in politics, even if you could not call your soul your own sufficiently to deal with him as the general interest dictates. And, believe me, the policy of our party so dictates, whatever may be your instructions from your immediate masters.' But I could multiply such letters into a volume and possibly other editors with greater virtue than I possess have not been neglected by these curious guardians of public morals."

44
Lady Aberdeen (1857-1939)

Ishbel Maria Gordon, Marchioness of Aberdeen and Temair, became in fact if not in name the country's first female governor general when her husband, Lord Aberdeen, was made vice-regent in 1893. In London, she had followed her mentor Gladstone's example in trying to assist prostitutes in their native habitat. In Ottawa, she attempted to turn Government House into a centre of social reform and to release the unrealised potential of Canadian women (she introduced to Canada the National Council of Women, for instance, and bucked the medical establishment to create the Victorian Order of Nurses). Which was all to the good particularly as Lord Aberdeen was as much renowned for his weakness and indecisiveness as she was for her strength and leadership. One of his important skills was imitating the sound of railway whistles. Another, a columnist of the day reported, was his success in "trying to look as if nobody was looking at him". Being the greater governor general of the family meant that Lady Aberdeen had to be the greater diplomat as well. She was, in contemporary nomenclature, a suffragist not a suffragette – that is, an effective practitioner of change, not a professional activist. When they were together in official situations, she could be seen "pulling on his sleeve, and offering suggestions".

45
Sir Joseph Flavelle (1858-1939)

As a millionaire pork-packer, Sir Joseph Flavelle was one of those who helped to make Toronto known as Hogtown. His name long carried a suggestion of scandal because of allegations, never proved, that the meat he supplied to Canadian troops in the First World War was tainted. With time, however, he has come to seem less of an individual devil and more part of an occupational stereotype: the eccentric capitalist, parsimonious and generous by turns, but consistently theatrical. It is recorded that on one early business trip he arrived at his destination late in the evening and slept on a bench in the railway station; innkeepers did not pro rate rooms and he saw no reason why he should have to pay for a full night's lodging if he were to be there only half a night. He enjoyed a spry old age (it was said that at seventy-three he could still catch houseflies with his bare hands). Perhaps he owed some of his health to the fact that he was a vigorous walker despite owning at various times a Rolls Royce, a Packard, and a Pierce-Arrow—in any event, expensive black cars; he was displeased when his niece began parking her yellow flivver in front of his mansion. He once sent his chauffeur to fetch one of his grandsons to the boardroom of the Bank of Commerce (another of his business interests). He accused the lad of being overdrawn in his account by three dollars. When it was shown to his satisfaction that this was not in fact the case, Sir Joseph treated the boy to a meal, a moving picture and a hockey game.

46
Andrew Bonar Law (1858-1923)

Many British Tories feared the worst when Bonar Law, a native of New Brunswick and an MP since 1900, succeeded the esteemed

Arthur Balfour as party leader in the House of Commons. John Buchan, for example, still seemed to suffer a chill of desperation when recalling the event thirty years later. In Buchan's view, Balfour "was the greatest public figure of that time. He was the only man in public life for whom I felt a disciple's loyalty. When he retired ... the glamour went out of politics for me, and my feeling was that of the current parody of the Prayer Book: 'Lord have mercy upon us and incline our hearts to Bonar Law.'" By 1915, Law held the first of a series of important cabinet portfolios and he became prime minister in 1922, the only Canadian, indeed the only colonial, ever to achieve that position. But he served only two hundred and nine days before resigning in ill health.

47

Sir Henry Pellatt (1859-1939)

The notorious Toronto capitalist, broker, sportsman and soldier is best remembered for Casa Loma, the grotesque ersatz castle he built for himself prior to the First World War. One of his neighbours, Lady Eaton, remembered the house-proud plutocrat giving her the tour:

"It was far from finished—in fact, much of the interior was never finished—but he and Lady Pellatt had made themselves comfortably at home in the east wing, and their huge conservatory was an enchanting place to linger in the evening as the lights came on, street by street, through the city far below.... For him the castle was more than life itself; certainly it was obvious to me following him around, up the twisting stone stairs, into the turrets, through the empty, echoing bedrooms, that he knew every detail of the design, the craftsmanship, and just as surely every effect he had hoped to achieve when he turned the first sod. When our tour was almost over and we were pausing in the corridor before a handsome carved oval frame that was still waiting for a painting, he said, 'I wish I had another million dollars. What do you think I would do with it?' There was hardly time for me to answer before he went on. 'I'd finish this house—and then die happy.'"

But it soon became a hotel when his fortunes took a nasty turn and a number of small investors went down with him. "Many people lost money in his manipulations," Lady Eaton continued, "but I have often heard it said—and having known him, I believe it—that no widow ever suffered by reason of Sir Henry's reverses. He took over such responsibilities even to his own detriment."

48
Sir Charles G.D. Roberts (1860-1943)

The famous poet and creator of animal stories was recognized as the virtual father of Canadian literature because of the attention he brought to the whole field by the international lustre of his own reputation. In certain circles, however, he was additionally renowned for his allegedly ravenous sexual appetites, though there is suspicion that this distinction, too, may have benefitted from his own efforts at ensuring its continuation. However, Kathleen Strange, an author of the day, provided Thomas Raddall with some firsthand testimony. She reported that Roberts would use the annual meetings of the Canadian Authors' Association as opportunities to seduce young women and that on one such occasion, apparently in the 1930s, he lured her to his hotel room with the promise of showing her, not etchings, but photographs of his bohemian days on the Continent. He passed her a series of pictures showing himself and Isadora Duncan in Grecian costume, though in less and less of it with each snapshot. The final print—depicting him *in puris naturalibus*—was accompanied by "a short struggle" that ended in a slap across his face. Strange went on to say that Sir Charles pointedly ignored her at the next several CAA conventions until, chancing upon her alone in a hotel corridor, he waxed magnanimous. "My deah," he said in his carefully groomed transatlantic accent, "I forgive you."

49

Ernest Thompson Seton (1860-1946)

Ernest Thompson Seton, the naturalist, illustrator and writer — whose book *Wild Animals I Have Known* should have been called *Wild Animals I Alone Have Known,* wags said — "left Canada with bitterness in his heart", according to Hector Charlesworth, who explained:

"Ernest Seton Thompson, or 'Thompson-Seton', as he later called himself, much to the indignation of his father ... spent his boyhood in Toronto, and the early nature stories that made him famous were based on eyewitness material that he collected in its environs and in Manitoba, where for a time, about 1890, he was government naturalist... He was almost the earliest of Canadian painters to treat the problems of snow in the analytic manner of the French impressionists. His chief picture was a large piece, 'Awaited in Vain,' which showed three wolves devouring the last remnants of a man they had slain. The time was evening, and the light in a distant hut showed the significance of the title. Though the subject was ghastly, and candidly handled, the beauty and veracity of the colour effect, the perfect painting of animals, gave the picture of haunting, sinister beauty I have never forgotten. The obvious cleverness of Thompson was rather disconcerting to his fellow painters. Shortly after, the assembling of paintings for the Canadian collection at the Chicago World's Fair began, and the jury of selection promptly rejected 'Awaited in Vain' on the grounds that it was too realistic and brutal. I was one of those who were convinced that that was not the real reason. Artists are as a class poor, and for that reason art politics sometimes get rather near the gutter. The painter of real brilliance

61

and originality who suddenly appears on the scene is apt to fare much as does the boy with a new suit of clothes who gets into a gang of urchins. So with my pen I made a fight for recognition for Ernest Thompson, and his other friends took up the cry. The result was that the jury of selection was forced by the government to reconsider its decision, and 'Awaited in Vain' went to Chicago. But when I saw it there some months later it had been hopelessly 'skyed' by the Canadian hanging committee. Thompson, who was a very handsome, slender young man, later spoiled his appearance by letting his hair grow too long, at the suggestion, it was said, of his lecture manager, who also may have been responsible for the change of name. Shortly after the episode just related he left Canada disgusted with the unkindness of his fellows..."

50

Sara Jeanette Duncan (1861-1922)

The author of *The Imperialist* and many other novels "had written a serial for the *Saturday Evening Post,* based on the theme of an imaginary marriage of a British Heir Apparent to an American girl. The story had such elements of popular interest in the United States, where every girl with a wealthy father is well aware that she is a Princess, that [the actress] Annie Russell, a really gifted artist, secured the right to produce a dramatic version. Miss Duncan thought that with her long experience as a fiction writer she was fully competent to write a play and stipulated that she should make her own dramatization. When the script was put into rehearsal it was found to be almost hopeless, bristling with lost opportunities to evoke dramatic interest and full of useless padding. But Miss Duncan insisted that it must remain unaltered, and though urged by experienced people like Miss Russell and the stage director, Eugene Presbrey, who knew immensely more about the theatre than herself, she refused all advice. The play was of course a 'flop' even when produced in friendly Canadian cities, and Miss Duncan thought herself an injured person."

51
E. Cora Hind (1861-1942)

Hind, a significant figure in the woman's suffrage movement, became the first important female journalist in western Canada when she began writing about agriculture in the Winnipeg *Free Press*. She would have acquired the distinction much earlier but on first applying for work on the paper in 1882 she had been rebuffed because of her gender (not the only such instance in her career). She had recently qualified as a typewriter (the word still referred to the operator of the machine, not the machine itself), and to support herself she became the first public stenographer west of the Great Lakes. Her clientele included local lawyers and businessmen as well as visiting dignitaries. Her most singular customer was a Spanish-speaking prospector who commissioned her to write a proposal of marriage to send to his English-speaking beloved in California. Hind recalled years afterward that as she applied herself to the chore she found herself wishing, if only for a moment, that she had read more romantic fiction. As it was, she blushed at the letter that rolled out of the carriage. "It was the most florid piece of literature I ever produced", she remembered. "My client said sadly that it was very cold, but that he supposed it would have to do."

52
Sir Edmund Wyly Grier (1862-1957)

A friendly contemporary ventured of Sir Edmund, the prolific painter of Canada's wealthy and high born, that he was "a master at the art of gentlemanly agreement and of precise expression. No one seems to recollect the time when Grier ever lost his temper. To lose temper is to forfeit one's balance, and Grier has a rather exquisite balance to maintain. He is an artillery major [First World War], a master of amateur gardening, [a] suffragist, an art critic, a dabbler in singing, and a cultivated Christian Scientist who used to be a not too orthodox Anglican."

To illustrate the clarity of disposition so essential to the portrait-painter's trade, the writer recalled how "Grier appeared at a restaurant luncheon among some friends one day a few years ago when there was a trifle of tight money in the studios and elsewhere. He was garbed for a wedding. To some of his friends' comments he naively asked, 'Yes, and where do you think I got these trousers? At Thompson's for a dollar-fifty.'

"Nobody but a master of temperamental equipose could have joked about a dollar-fifty pair of trousers at a fashionable wedding."

53
E. Pauline Johnson (1862-1913)

Nine days before her death, the Indian princess, poet and platform entertainer, the author of *Flint and Feather*, *Legends of Vancouver* and other works suitable for bindings of limp leather, wrote her last will and testament. It stipulated that her body "not be taken east" but that she be cremated in or near Vancouver while "dressed in my grey cloth evening cloak, with my small gold shield-shaped locket (containing the photograph of a young boy) fastened round my neck by the small gold chain." The survivors who carried out her wishes did not open the locket to look at the photograph. Years earlier, however, Johnson had shown the picture to a friend whom she swore to secrecy; the friend remembered it as a likeness of a man rather than of a boy but did not learn his identity.

Nor has anyone learned it since. Johnson's biographer has speculated on a long list of males who were important in the poet's life and concluded that the "only one who cannot be ruled completely out" is in that position "partly because so little is known about him."

54
Arthur Ellis (1864-1936?)

Ellis, whose real name was Arthur Bartholomew English, was Canada's official hangman; so great an impression did he make in his long career that all subsequent holders of the office took the name Arthur Ellis as well. He was, of necessity perhaps, an elusive figure, but Frederick Griffin, the Toronto journalist, left the following account after he "spent two hours with him in his hotel bedroom in Woodstock, Ontario, one May night in 1921, where he was waiting to hang a murderer named Garfield.

"It was a thundery evening and our talk was punctuated with flashes of lightning which, always a romantic, I found a setting properly sinister. I was interested, not disgusted, when once, with a friendly gesture, he placed his hand around my shoulder. Yet I shuddered, for that hand had thus gone around the shoulders of two hundred men and women whom he said he had hanged [six hundred was his career-total]. At dawn it would go around the shoulders of Garfield.

"Whatever is the popular conception of a hangman, Ellis did not fit. Seen on the street, he was a small, meek-appearing, yet jaunty figure, for all the world like a deacon on his way to church, carrying a pair of neatly folded black kid gloves. Though inconspicuous and incognito, he gave no hint of furtiveness as a tradesman of death. Indeed, a Bible under his arm was all that he needed to make him seem a figure of confident piety. Later, in his bedroom, seen close-up, this feeling of him as a religious person strengthened. He had the thin, nervous, tight-lipped face of a zealot. He spoke clearly, almost gently, with a Lancashire accent, and with a decided sense of drama, using his forefinger for emphasis. Weak eyes behind heavy glasses were his only, shall I say? ghoulish feature. They had an effect of death, as if they were not eyes, but empty sockets – this again may have been merely my imagination.

"In general, he had an air of not quite belonging to this generation, as if he had stepped out of the pages of *Barnaby Rudge*.

"'I never take a liberty in a prison,' he said, 'and I never allow one.'

"He was vain, an exquisite, with two heavy rings on his left hand, a massive gold watch chain and a tiny black bow tie perched at the front of a high, stiff, double collar; yet he fascinated, and entertained. He could laugh at himself and his job as he told of seeing in an hotel a man pointed out as the hangman and shunned. 'Poor fellow!' he said. 'He had my sympathy.'

"'In carrying out the extreme sentence of the law,' he declared oracularly, 'I am the last wheel and the smallest wheel. The judge sanctions the execution; I merely perform it. I take it very religiously.'

"'How do you mean, religiously?' I asked.

"'I mean sacredly, rather,' he said, his eyes glowing like dark fires, so that for all his unction I shrank from him. 'It is a solemn, a sacred duty. But no, I make no special preparations. On a day of execution, I may be a little more serious, concentrated, I think you'd call it – that is all.'

"He liked books, he said, especially history, and his favourite author was Marie Corelli. He got off this aphorism: 'There is not as much pain in being hanged as in having a tooth pulled.' Maybe he was right at that; there is no ache afterwards."

Ellis remained a staunch advocate of capital punishment to the end, but came out in favour of the electric chair over the gallows, declaring that the new technology was safer.

55
Thomas P. (Doc) Kelley (1864-1930)

The career of Mack Sennett (1884-1960), the Canadian who created the vogue for slapstick film comedies, could not have taken place without the effort of his fellow countryman Doc Kelley, the proprietor of a prominent travelling medicine show. For it was in Newfoundland in 1889 that Kelley observed a hotel stable boy being chased by the establishment's cook, who brandished a piece of pie. The lad turned to plead with his pursuer, who flung the pie at him. Two layabouts observing the scene broke out laughing. A companion of Kelley's suggested that Newfoundlanders would laugh at anything, but Kelley was deep in thought. "Instead of hitting his shirt and making a few blotches, what if that boy had been hit in the face?" he asked aloud. "And not by a bit of pie? How about a whole pie, big and juicy, deliberately and carefully pushed smack into his face... How long do you think these folks would laugh then?" And so was born the cream-pie-in-the-face school of comedy.

56
Henry Marshall Tory (1864-1947)

Marshall, a scientist as well as an educator, holds the unusual and perhaps unique distinction of having helped to found three universities—UBC, the University of Alberta and Carleton. Or four, if you count the so-called Khaki University established in England for the benefit of Canadian troops during the First World War. At some point in his own schooling he had learned to knit. As part of the war effort that began in 1914, he taught the skill to professors' wives at the U of A so that they could make socks and caps for the soldiers. "Dr. and Mrs. Tory did not dance," one observer recalled, "so the faculty women used to bring their knitting and hand it to Dr. Tory to have him turn the heel properly. By the end of the evening he would always have the job done."

57
George Weston (1864-1924)

The founder of the Weston food empire, the father of Garfield Weston and the grandfather of Galen Weston, died in a singular fashion. He was "felled by pneumonia incurred, according to legend, when he walked miles through a blizzard rather than spend money for cabfare or overnight accommodation."

58
Sir Lyman Poore Duff (1865-1955)

Sir Lyman Duff sat on the Supreme Court of Canada for nearly forty years, latterly as chief justice, and was acknowledged as the most distinguished jurist Canada ever produced. Perhaps his most enduring decision was that which upheld the Dominion's action in abolishing the right of appeal to the Privy Council in London (thus making the Supreme Court as an institution, and he himself, more powerful).

He was a curious figure whose drinking problem (which his biographer believes may have stemmed from impotence) almost got him dismissed from the bench. Other eccentricities had a legalistic foundation. What at first often appeared to be the bad habit of talking to himself was, in reality, his way of settling points of law in his own mind. One contemporary recalled him walking all alone down the corridor to his chambers, muttering, "Tilley, what do you take me for, a damned fool? That's arrant nonsense. I don't believe any of it...." A waiter at the Rideau Club once saw him pacing "vigorously up and down engaged in a most animated discussion with some unseen companion, gesticulating all the while and punctuating his strongest remarks with gestures, presumably appropriate to the point he was making at the time [and] postulating arguments to both sides of a question — taking first the plaintiff's [and] then the defendant's." But no one disputed his brilliant mind or amazing memory. The Ontario attorney-general's office once sought his help in an archival matter, hoping he might have some knowledge of a memorandum about escheats (the reversion of property to the Crown) that had been written in 1875. He sat down at once and wrote a letter indicating in what book the information could be located and apologizing for not recalling the page number. Before he could finish, the page number came back to him and he included it in a post scriptum.

59
J.W. Dafoe (1866-1944)

The voice of Western liberalism was apparently capable of some lighter moments during his infrequent absences from the editor's chair of the Winnipeg *Free Press,* which he occupied for forty-three years. He could report from Bermuda during a stay there in 1931 that he had "paid some attention to the rum swizzlers [whose] component parts are rum, grapefruit juice, ice, brown Demerara sugar and a dash of bitters." So powerful was the mixture, he contended, that after several samples "at a party last Sunday a Scotch-Canadian ... hailed me as his long lost brother and called me John."

60
Emily Murphy (1868-1933)

Murphy was a popular journalist who often used the *nom de plume* Janey Canuck. Not long after removing to Alberta from Ontario in 1903, she heard the story of a married woman left penniless when her husband of eighteen years sold their farm and ran off to the United States with another woman. Murphy led the campaign that resulted in the Gower Act of 1911, under which women were entitled to one-third of their husbands' property. It was but one of her many drives for reform both within and without the suffragist movement. As she once remarked, "Whenever I don't know whether to fight or not—I fight!" She was a virulent anti-drug crusader, for example, and was one of four women who instigated the famous Persons Case (in which the Privy Council in London ruled in 1929 that Canadian women were legally persons under the BNA Act).

In 1916, when members of an Edmonton women's group claimed status as observers at the trial of several girls on morals charges, the magistrate banished them from the proceedings, saying that the testimony about to be heard should not fall on womanly years. Murphy commenced a campaign for female magistrates and was soon made the first such one in the Empire, though she was only self-taught in the law. She defended the appointment by quoting a friend to the effect that rearing children gives one considerable experience in judging cases of "false pretenses, assault incitement, breach of peace, cruelty to animals, cheating at play, loitering, appropriation, false evidence, trespass, idle and disorderly persons, and many other offences" of the sort common in police court. Her first day on the bench, she reported, was a nervous time for everyone present. "All the men became embarrassed and started to stammer over their manner of addressing me. One said 'Your Worship' and another 'Your Honour.' A negro said 'Your Majesty' and the rest said 'Sir.'"

61
Robbie Ross (1868-1918)

Ross was the first homosexual lover, and the lifelong defender, of Oscar Wilde. His maternal grandfather was Robert Baldwin, the co-premier of Upper Canada following the establishment of responsible government, and his father was in Baldwin's cabinet. As a very young man Ross had been beaten for reading Wilde's poems. When the two actually met, at Oxford in 1886, Wilde characterised him as having "the face of Puck". Two years later he entered King's College, Cambridge, but had a short and unhappy stay: he caught pneumonia after being dumped in the fountain by a group of students who objected to an article he had written in the *Granta,* the student literary magazine. He was with Wilde at the time of his arrest on charges of committing indecent acts, but though he himself avoided prosecution he was ostracized in some quarters. He never wavered in his loyalty to Wilde, however, and after Wilde's death in exile in 1900 expressed the wish that his own ashes might be placed in Wilde's tomb in Pere Lachaise cemetery in Paris. This request was carried out in 1950.

62
Stephen Leacock (1869-1944)

This most popular and prolific of Canadian writers was also by all accounts one of the worst dressed. Around McGill University, where he taught for thirty-three years, he was a familiar figure even at a distance, owing to his tattered academic gown, which was often bedecked with ashes from his pipe, or his moth-eaten raccoon coat, which went on year after year lacking several of its buttons. These outer garments, however, hid even greater eccentricity beneath, much of it apparently due to Leacock's absence of mind.

Not only was the watch-chain stretched across his waistcoat mended with one or more safety pins, it often supported his latchkey, so that he would not forget to carry it and thus lock himself out of his home. Once, after he had been interrupted midway through dressing for dinner, he descended the stairs half in formal dress and half in loud checks. His mother-in-law suggested that there would be no fear of embarrassment should Leacock lose his trousers in some accident since he was likely to be wearing a second pair under the first. But her theory was never tested because when Leacock could not immediately locate a belt he would take the precaution of using a necktie or even a piece of rope to hold up his trousers. Also, he was known frequently to wear two hats at the same time, one jammed inside the other.

Sir Arthur Currie, the principal of McGill, was the host of an important dinner party to which Leacock arrived very late and not quite in a complete state of dress. "Lady Curry," he asked the hostess, "would you tie my tie? My niece, Barbara, is out." Lady Curry did as requested and, turning, introduced him to the guest of honour, Lord Bessborough, the governor general.

63
R.B. Bennett (1870-1947)

The man who would become prime minister of Canada and ultimately Viscount Bennett moved to Calgary in 1897 to join a law firm closely associated with the Canadian Pacific Railway. Soon he was playing host to daily luncheons at a special table in the Alberta Hotel. Across the dining room was the rival table presided over by Bob Edwards,

the editor and publisher of the *Eye Opener*. That brave but scur-
rilous journal was soon conducting a campaign of "ridicule and
awkward truth" against both Bennett and the railway. Edwards was
sincere in hating the CPR's monopolistic practices but got the point
across to his readers by dwelling on safety conditions at the local
rail crossings. He reported every possible accident at outrageous
length and in embarrassing detail. When there was no accident to
describe, he contented himself with pointing out that "Not a life was
lost or a buggy smashed at the C.P.R. crossing last week." One
memorable edition carried three front-page photographs labelled
"Recent C.P.R. Wrecks in Alberta". Inside was a portrait of Bennett
labelled "Another C.P.R. Wreck". There is reason to suppose that
in 1906 it was Edwards' persistent attacks that cost Bennett a seat
in the legislature of the newly formed province, even though he was
by then leader of its Conservative party.

Inevitably, friends and colleagues of the two antagonists were
drawn into the feud. Edwards' closest associate was a local lawyer,
Patrick Nolan. One day Nolan and Bennett squared off against each
other in court. Bennett was bolstering his case by hurling a large
number of precedents at the judge, saying to his law clerk, "Boy,
give me Phipson on Evidence" or "Boy, give me Kenny on Crimes."
When it came Nolan's turn, he rose and said, "Boy, get me Bennett
on Boloney."

As his political ambitions grew, Bennett tried mightily to win over
Edwards and his newspaper. It looked as though he had succeeded
when he persuaded Edwards to attend a Conservative banquet at
which he, Bennett, was officiating. Bennett extended Edwards the
honour of saying grace. But after a long silence Edwards declined,
saying, "If you don't mind, Mr. Chairman, I'd prefer that the good
Lord didn't know I was here."

64

"Bennett was a man of mood who seldom caught the ear of the House. As an orator he was powerful rather than persuasive. Meighen could run rings around him. In politics Bennett was a combination of Billy Graham and Jack the Ripper.

"Bennett was impressed by pomp and ceremony. Like King he had a curious reverence for the opposite sex: his mother and his sister Mildred, a rather jolly, dashing woman, held a high place in his affections. He liked older women. He had a burning desire to hold centre stage and was always deeply moved at recognition accorded some poor but deserving person, no doubt a symbol of his own early frustrations. On one occasion, the consecration of Cardinal Villeneuve at the Basilica in Quebec City, Bennett's eyes filled with tears when the Cardinal's father was led down the main aisle to a front pew."

65

One day in 1932, when he was the editor of *Saturday Night,* Hector Charlesworth was startled to discover a novel suggestion in an unsolicited manuscript that had lain unread on his desk for some time. The article "proved an almost intolerable rigmarole relating to biblical prophecies. Hon. Mr. Aberhart of Alberta would perhaps have found it light and pleasant reading but it was too deep for me. However, toward the last page or two its purpose was revealed. Nothing less than this; that the world's troubles would not be solved until anti-Christ appeared and started the Battle of Armageddon. The writer assumed, as do most of those who look forward to the joys of Armageddon, that anti-Christ would be defeated and then the Millenium would begin. The writer was logical in his contention that somebody to play the role of anti-Christ was a *sine qua non,* of the whole situation. And then came the momentous suggestion that Richard Bedford Bennett should accept the responsibility, proclaim himself anti-Christ, get Armageddon under way and thus precipitate the Millenium. A letter attached to the script revealed the thought that I had sufficient influence with Mr. Bennett to induce him to make the sacrifice if I backed my request with a public appeal in the Press."

Knowing that Bennett's "sense of humour was being over-taxed by the problems with which he had to deal" in Ottawa, Charlesworth did not follow the suggestion, but mentioned the proposal to a person he knew who was "an authority on the prophets and also the Book of Revelation [and] familiar with [such matters as the] measurements of the Great Pyramid, that have in latter years become tied up in some way which I do not understand with Armageddon and the subsequent Millenium." The man replied that the writer of the manuscript was crazy. "Nobody in Canada has the slightest chance of recognition as anti-Christ", he explained. "Anti-Christ will come from somewhere in the Balkans. In my opinion he will be here soon, and the prophecies show that he will be mixed up with the gold standard."

Thus, reported Charlesworth, "though Mr. Bennett's belief in the gold standard might be a recommendation, other circumstances were against him, and his chance to shine universally in a role entirely different from that of Prime Minister of Canada was to all intents and purposes *nil*."

66
Emily Carr (1871-1945)

Emily Carr was routinely mocked for the very elements which combine to form her greatness as a painter—her relationship with the British Columbia rain forests, her response to the native culture, her insistence on supporting herself modestly by teaching and potting rather than be distracted by any sort of commerce. Her love of animals was taken as an especially clear sign of eccentricity rather than as further proof of her humanity.

In a studio with many dogs, cats and other small mammals (and birds), her monkey, Woo, always enjoyed a special place. Her companion Carol Pearson recalled that the artist made the creature "little house coats open down the back instead of the front... Miss Carr would hold Woo between her knees as she stitched the dress on, using a strong string. When the monkey, unable to get out of the dress, tired of pulling, Miss Carr would reward her by putting some of her favourite candy in the little pocket, which had had to be nearly welded on! In this way Woo gradually learned to respect the pocket, and after some time the dresses were made with buttons; the battle was won."

Carr (who also sewed her own shroud so as to spare her next of kin the trouble) saved old shoes and put them in the garden as nests for the field mice, stuffing a fragment of woolen sock into each. When the autumn cold drove the mice indoors, she would kill them only with great reluctance and special consideration. In addition to the securely tied-down bit of cheese used as bait, she would lay another piece on the floor next to the mousetrap. That way, she explained, no mouse would die hungry or with unfulfilled expectations.

67
Roald Amundsen (1872-1928)

"Amundsen in the late nineties accomplished one feat of importance to Canada which passed almost unnoticed. He was the first mariner to run the Northwest passage from the Arctic Ocean to the Pacific. All through the mid-nineteenth century British scientists and explorers discussed the possibility of finding the Northwest passage, and on that quest Sir John Franklin lost his life. Yet when Amundsen actually accomplished the feat, the world was so occupied with other matters that it attracted little attention, and he did not actually become famous until he discovered the South Pole."

68
Hector Charlesworth (1872-1945)

The celebrated editor and critic became the first head of the Canadian Radio Broadcasting Commission, the forerunner of the CBC, and so came within reach of politics, as when on the floor of Parliament "the famous Jean-François Pouliot, M.P. for Temiscouata, whose sword is always loose in the scabbard, especially distinguished himself. 'Mr. Charlesworth's tongue should be torn from his mouth and wound seven times around his whiskers,' was one of his flights.

"This was too much for Felix Quinn, M.P. for Halifax (now a Senator), who, apparently fed up, suddenly ejaculated, 'Sit down, you jackass!' As Mr. Quinn is a quiet type of Irishman, who seldom speaks, his interjection caused great surprise and the House was in an uproar. The Prime Minister rose and said that the debate was not of a character to bring credit on the House. Mr. Quinn at once withdrew his remark, and there were demands that Mr. Pouliot withdraw his offensive reference to myself. Mr. Pouliot was not under compulsion to do so, because a member of Parliament is at liberty to say anything he pleases about anybody save fellow members, and he retorted, 'I will withdraw when he shaves off his beard.' Armand Lavergne, Deputy Speaker, who was in the Chair made a dry remark suggesting that members preserve the atmosphere of a gentleman's club, and the incident closed. Later I met Mr. Pouliot at a social gathering, and asked him to take a good look at me. He at once became friendly and our personal relations were excellent from then on."

69
Nellie McClung (1873-1951)

"I remember one day when I was leaving for a ten-day lecture tour I bought an Accident Insurance Policy for five thousand dollars at the railway wicket, paying two dollars and a half for ten days' insurance", wrote the famous western feminist and author. "I had often done this before but had never really read the blue slip which I had received. But on this day I went over it carefully. It contained some excellent clauses, all beginning: 'If the insured be male.' It told how much he would be paid in case of total disability, partial disability, the loss of a hand or a foot or an eye, but always the sentence began in that ominous way: 'If the insured be male.' I wondered what the company had for me. On the other side of the slip I found it. In a little enclosure, fenced off in black, as if someone were already dead, appeared this inscription:

"'Females are insured against death only.'

"When I went back to the office I sought out the man who had sold me the policy and laid the matter before him.

"'Why is it,' I asked, 'that you take a woman's money and give her lower protection than you give men?'

"He said he didn't know anything about it, but he would find somebody who might know. The next man assured me that he didn't know that women ever bought accident policies. He didn't know they could buy them, but he would take me in to see Mr. Brown; Mr. Brown would know. Mr. Brown did know. Mr. Brown knew so well he was rather impatient with me for asking.

"'Don't you know,' said Mr. Brown severely, taking off his glasses, as if to let his brain cool, 'that women are much more highly sensitized than men, and would be more easily hurt in an accident, they would be a victim of pure nerves, would like nothing better than to lie in bed for a week or two, and draw her seven-fifty a week.

They would think they were hurt when they really were not, and there would be no end of trouble.'

"'But, Mr. Brown,' I said, 'what about the clause relating to the loss of hand or foot? You would not be altogether dependent on the woman's testimony in that, would you? You could check them up—if they are pretending, could you not?'

"Mr. Brown's face indicated that he couldn't be bothered answering any more foolish questions. He put on his glasses, and I knew I was being dismissed. I thanked Mr. Brown for his information and told him that I hoped to have an opportunity of bringing the matter before the next convention of insurance men.

"Mr. Brown looked up then quickly.

"'Have the insurance men invited you to speak to them?' he asked sharply.

"'No,' I answered truthfully. 'They haven't. But they will.'"

70
William Lyon Mackenzie King (1874-1950)

Too much has been made already of Mackenzie King's interest in spiritualism, as though it were proof *ipso facto* of a closed mind and not an indication of the opposite. It must be admitted, however, that some of the results of his enquiries, which included the use of ouija boards and tea leaves as well as psychic mediums, are vivid testimony to his credulity. Witness King's own record of a seance involving himself, his friend Joan Patteson (who "filled the place of my mother in my heart") and the spirit of his maternal grandfather William Lyon Mackenzie, the rebel, who had died in 1861.

Mackenzie told his descendant, "You were predestined to be Prime Minister at this time... The fate of Canada is in your hands, the fate of Great Britain depends on Canada, the fate of Europe depends on Great Britain...."

"Go on, Mackenzie", King urged.

Joan Patteson was unable to suppress a laugh but made up for the lapse by using an honorific, saying "Go on, Mr. Mackenzie."

"Mrs. Patteson is more polite than you are", the spirit remarked.

"I was speaking historically", replied the grandson.

The conversation, if that is the proper term, took place in 1936 shortly after the Abdication Crisis. Late in 1939, Mackenzie was warning King about Hitler, though somewhat redundantly so, since Hitler by then had already invaded Poland.

Indeed it is hard to escape the conclusion that Mackenzie was much better served by his many living advisors than by his equally numerous dead ones. In 1933, for instance, the Conservatives had restored the custom of allowing Canadians to be included in the King's New Year's honours list, a practice that had been suspended after the First World War when so many oleaginous robber barons had been transformed into robber baronets. Mackenzie's long-dead father claimed to have the inside track and supplied a list of who the new knights would be — Vincent Massey, for example. But when the official announcement was made, it included none of those names, only two scientists, Frederick Banting (who in time would be another King confidant from the Beyond) and Charles Saunders, the developer of Marquis wheat. Sir Wilfrid Laurier (died 1919) seems to have been especially generous in supplying King with disinformation from the Other Side. Not all such resource persons were Canadian, however. Dr Louis Pasteur (died 1895) went so far as to prescribe medicine for King's dog. Sometimes the spirit communiques must have become a sort of bureaucratic intrusion upon what was already a hectic schedule. One day in 1947, King noted in his diary that talks with Franklin Delano Roosevelt "took up most of the morning." President Roosevelt had been dead since 1945.

As a young man, Mackenzie King worked briefly as a reporter on the Toronto *Globe,* where "he held somewhat aloof from his colleagues, though I think this was not deliberate but rather the result of a temperamental difference. They tell one story about him, and I believe that, upon rare occasions of expansion, he tells it upon himself. Toronto newspapers were making much of the mysterious disappearance of a young woman. Armed with a description of the girl, King set forth from the *Globe* office in a spirit of high resolve. He would find her or perish in the attempt. The first day he had no luck, although he walked many miles of streets and gazed somewhat boldly into the faces of great numbers of pedestrians. But on the afternoon of the second day he came upon a young lady who seemed to fulfil the police description in all particulars. Approaching this damsel, the reporter invited her to accompany him. The damsel accepted, with suggestive alacrity, and in a few minutes, probably to her great surprise, found herself in the *Globe* office. King was explaining the triumphant issue of his search when the City Editor, a hard-boiled person, emerged from his sanctum. He looked at King and he looked at the girl. The latter he dismissed, curtly and decisively. To the future Prime Minister he said: 'King, if you ever again bring a prostitute into this office you're fired.'"

72

Arthur Meighen (1874-1960)

Canada's ninth prime minister once appeared in the House of Commons shod in carpet slippers. Also, he was unnaturally fond of a tatty old overcoat he had worn for years, perhaps decades. The garment was such a disgrace that once, when they were travelling by train, a group of his friends removed it from its hook and threw it out of the window. A railway employee found it, identified it and returned it to its owner, who continued to wear it for several more years.

73
Robert W. Service (1874-1958)

When "The Shooting of Dan McGrew" and other works made him prosperous, "the Poet of the Yukon" adopted a rich lifestyle, replete with fast company and unhealthy habits. Later, to correct the imbalance, he took to weight-lifting and other extreme forms of exercise. During a medical examination in 1924, when he was fifty, he gave the doctor an account of a typical day: two hours in the gym, then swimming, then a three-hour hike, followed in the evening by some vigorous boxing in preparation for an upcoming match. The doctor interrupted.

"What's the matter?" Service asked.

"The motor's the matter. Running a hundred to the minute. Stuttering too. Leaky valve. Backfire."

Service asked him what he meant.

"Your heart. It's as big as that of an ox, and *it whistles*."

"But I never felt so fit in my life."

"I don't doubt it. All the same you're killing yourself. Slow suicide...."

The doctor prescribed moderation, which the patient embraced with his usual extremism. By 1928, he was publishing a book, *Why Not Grow Young? Or Living for Longevity*, outlining his method of life extension. He lived to be eighty-four.

John Buchan, 1st Baron Tweedsmuir (1875-1940)

In 1935, John Buchan, the Scottish parliamentarian and popular writer of mystery novels such as *The Thirty-Nine Steps,* was appointed Canadian vice-regent. "It was considered necessary that the new Governor-General-elect should be raised to the peerage, as he was to represent the King as formal ruler of the great Dominion. The question necessarily arose of what his title should be. His own surname, which he had made famous, was inadmissible, since there was already an Earldom of Buchan in existence. He had himself always cherished a secret fancy that if ever he became a peer he would call himself Lord Manorwater, taking his title from the little moorland water that runs into Tweed two miles above Peebles. (The name appealed to him so much it appears more than once in his writings; for instance, the story 'The Company of the Marjolaine' in *The Moon Endureth* is supposed to be an 'extract from the unpublished papers of the Manorwater family'.) However, Mr. Mackenzie King, who was consulted as to the suitability of the title Lord Manorwater, gave it as his opinion that it was inadvisable, and John Buchan chose instead the name of Tweedsmuir, a tiny village on the upper course of Tweed...."

The death of George V in January 1936 meant that many events were cancelled as the court went into mourning for a year. Accordingly, Tweedsmuir's first months at Rideau Hall were quiet, with the result that both he and Lady Tweedsmuir wrote novels. In time, however, he was caught up in the rounds of official duties, principally speeches, and "he was irked a little by the fact that the Governor-General was prohibited by his position from making any remark that might be regarded as in any degree controversial; he wittily described the sort of remarks that it was permissible for him to make as 'Governor-Generalities'."

He travelled the country much more widely than any of his predecessors, and in 1937 explored the far north. "At every trading-post on the [Mackenzie] river he stopped and met all the inhabitants. On 28 July he arrived at [Aklavik], the ultimate edge of civilization [and] from there he made a flight in a Royal Canadian Air Force machine out over the delta to Tuko-Yaktuk, and visited that Eskimo settlement on the shore of the Arctic Ocean. On the return journey fog came down and the pilot lost his way; it was the Governor-General who saved them both by his skill in map-reading."

75

Tweedsmuir suffered a fall at Rideau Hall and lay unconscious for four days as his aides fed releases to a hungry press corps. Finally it was decided that Dr Wilder Penfield, the world-famous Montreal neurosurgeon, should operate in order to relieve the pressure on the governor-general's brain. An operating room was set up at Government House before plans were revised and Tweedsmuir was removed to Montreal aboard a special train. Four operations in as many days failed to save him, for "a clot which had formed in his leg led to a pulmonary embolism and his heart stopped beating. For over an hour the surgical team tried desperately to resuscitate him but without success. The final official bulletin, released at 7:20 P.M. stated simply, 'The Governor-General died at 7:13 P.M.'

"At the [Montreal Neurological] Institute, despite the fact that everything possible had been done for Tweedsmuir, depression set in."

76
General Sir Arthur Currie (1875-1933)

An old school friend recalled years later that the First World War commander had shown an aptitude for strategy even as an adolescent in Strathroy, Ontario. On one occasion, Currie was the final speaker in a closely fought debate and was allowed five minutes to conclude his team's argument. When the allotment expired, the referee called time, but Currie continued debating. The judge again ordered him to stop. But Currie knew that under a strict interpretation of the rules he could finish his sentence before sitting down. So he left the stage and slowly circumambulated the auditorium before returning, finally, to his seat, with "slow, short, and deliberate steps" and "shooting arguments like bullets". He concluded his last point at the very moment his posterior was reunited with the chair. According to a modern biographer, "This is an early indication of Currie's fierce determination to win and his coolness under pressure", qualities that played a part in his conduct at Vimy Ridge, after which he was knighted in the field by King George.

77

Tom Thomson (1877-1917)

Dr James M. MacCallum, the Toronto physician who became the patron and champion of the Group of Seven, was in J.E.H. Mac-Donald's studio one day when "the door opened and in walked a tall and slim, clean-cut, dark young chap who was introduced to me as Tom Thomson. Quiet, chary of words, he impressed me as full of resolution and independence.

"After he had gone, I told MacDonald of how I had heard of him and asked him to get some of his sketches so that I might get an idea of what the country was like. This was done, and as I looked them over, I, who had known the north since the days when Collingwood and Orillia were railheads, realised their truthfulness, their feeling and their sympathy for the grim fascinating northland. Dark they were, muddy in color, tight, and not wanting in technical defects but they made me feel that the North had gripped Thomson as it had gripped me when as a boy of eleven, I first sailed and paddled through its silent places.

"Some of the sketches, fished out from the foot of the rapids, I bought. The money was received with the remark: 'That will let me buy some more paint.'"

78
William (Bible Bill) Aberhart (1878-1943)

In 1932, Aberhart, the radio evangelist who had broken away from the Baptists to begin his own fundamentalist sect, was born yet again when he converted to Social Credit. In 1935, he gave Alberta the world's first Social Credit government and promptly began putting into practice the bizarre economic ideas on which the party was based. The most important of these was distribution of so-called prosperity certificates to the citizenry: free money with which people were to shore up the capitalist structure, whose future, in the middle of the Depression, seemed none too certain. In fact, Aberhart was no visionary but an economic naif who blindly went about wrecking what was left of Alberta's credit.

In 1936, he granted an interview, but reluctantly, to the editor of *The Financial Post*. "We Albertans are the richest people in the world", he stated. "We have three billion tons of coal in this province. What do you pay for coal in Toronto? Ten dollars a ton? All right, if we were to capitalize our coal at $10, we'd have $30 billion. There are 700,000 people in Alberta, so figure it out for yourself how wealthy each Albertan would be if we capitalized our natural resources."

The editor responded by pointing out that in Toronto he also paid fifty cents for a block of ice and that if the fewer than ten thousand Canadian Eskimos were to capitalize their own natural resources they would easily be the richest people on earth.

Lord Beaverbrook (1879-1964)

In his twilight years, the Fleet Street press baron and political power broker, who was born in Ontario and made his first fortune in Montreal, began to take an inordinate interest in New Brunswick, where he had spent his youth and adolescence. He gave the town of Newcastle the manse once occupied by his father, a Presbyterian minister; it became a public library consisting only of books of which Beaverbrook approved. Newcastle responded by commissioning a Beaverbrook bust. His largesse was most obvious in Fredericton, where he built the Lord Beaverbrook Art Gallery, whose local supporters then erected a statue of him not too far distant from a Beaverbrook bust paid for by the citizenry at large. He often toyed with the notion of buying a house in Fredericton but contented himself with space in the Lord Beaverbrook Hotel (which he did not build but merely allowed to be named after him) as well as an apartment kept for his use in the basement of the gallery. In 1961, his biographer A.J.P. Taylor travelled with him to Fredericton on business relating to the University of New Brunswick, another of his causes. Taylor recalls that Beaverbrook maintained a lively interest in academic affairs, "in particular harassing the Vice-Chancellor and some of the professors." Malcolm Muggeridge, when he was the principal book reviewer of Beaverbrook's *Evening Standard*, published an article in *Maclean's* suggesting that in Fredericton "memorials to the Beaver outnumber churches". But Muggeridge was mistaken for this merely seemed to be the case. His contract with the *Standard* was allowed to lapse.

80
Mazo de la Roche (1879-1961)

Once, late in her long career, the author of the *Jalna* novels submitted a short story to *The Tamarack Review,* a literary magazine. The editors agreed to decline it, and the manuscript was returned with the insincere expressions of gratitude common in such situations. "I'm not surprised that you didn't like the story", she wrote in reply. "Caroline [Clement, her companion] didn't like it, and I didn't like it very much myself, but as I've never liked any of the stories in *Tamarack,* I thought it might do very well."

81
Ernest Jones (1879-1958)

Jones, one of the important early disciples of Sigmund Freud and the author of a famous three-volume Freud biography, came to Toronto from Britain in 1908 to take up positions at the University of Toronto and the local hospital for the insane. There can be few such sojourns that have ended in greater acrimony. Jones disliked Canadians instinctively, reporting to Freud, in one of his four hundred letters to the Master, that they were "naive, childish and [held only] the simplest views of the problems of life." Business and sport were their only concerns, he went on, and the level of public discussion abysmal. In a particularly damning indictment, he stated that Canadians chewed gum rather than smoking or drinking. He found patently absurd the assumption that Canadian civilisation is based on a merger of the British and American varieties while avoiding the evil extremes of both.

Relations were reciprocal. The prickly former Harley Street practitioner lived in Brunswick Avenue with his sister and his mistress in what looked suspiciously like a *menage à trois*. He was accused (for the third time in his career) of having an *affaire* with a patient, though the charge was not proved. And he apparently alienated his colleagues both by shirking his teaching duties and monopolizing a learned journal that came under his control. One of his articles described, in detail that many found insufficiently clinical, a woman who believed that the Bible commanded her to engage in oral sex. Jones's diagnosis was the sort which in more recent years has won for Freudian analysis a place beside evangelism and TV wrestling. He suggested that she suffered from hypomania and nymphomania. There were rumblings of possible questions in the House of Commons.

But then Jones's stay was marked by a tangle of threats, insults, promises of lawsuits and fear of private investigators. At length, his presence proved too much for the university and in 1913 he moved on.

82
Vilhjalmur Stefansson (1879-1962)

Stefansson's work as an Arctic explorer convinced him that most talk about the need for a balanced diet was nonsense, that human beings could be quite healthy if they ate nothing but meat. To prove the point, he and a colleague began an experiment in 1927. For a period of a year, half of it spent in Bellevue Hospital in New York, they ate nothing but meat—once they had first gone a while on a more normal diet, to prove the contrast. They took in between 2600 and 2800 calories per day, derived eighty per cent from fat and twenty per cent from lean meat. At the end of twelve months, the men showed no more evidence of arteriosclerosis, high blood pressure, kidney damage or any other such problem than they had done previously. Stefansson was pleased. "To me this had been an anthropological and physiological study, and in it I was not impartial", he wrote. Nor was his sponsor, the American Meat Institute.

83
Louis Hémon (1880-1913)

Hémon was the French immigrant who wrote *Marie Chapdelaine,* the stark and simple story of rural French Canadian life. The book first appeared in 1914—after its author, who was temporarily deaf, had been killed by a train whose approach he could not hear. Its subsequent critical and financial success in English in the early 1920s prompted a Toronto journalist to go to the Lac St Jean region, about two hundred miles north of Quebec City, searching for the persons on whom the various characters were based. One of them was Samuel Bédard, who described crossing the lake by steamer one day in 1912 with a party of other settlers.

"To one side, aloof but interested, anxious to hear yet diffident of intrusion, was a slight man of thirty-two, a stranger, obviously not a pioneer....

"Bédard, curious, inquisitive, strolled over and began to chat. The Frenchman turned eagerly to question him. The latter offered, slyly, to sell him his farm.

"'No,' said Hémon, 'I do not seek to buy land but I have a proposal, my friend. I should like to work for you.'

"'You mean, help on the farm, clear land? But you are not a colonist, not a workman!'

"'I am willing, and if you agree I will come with you for eight dollars a month.'"

Hémon made only one condition, "that he should have Saturday afternoons free. At other times he played the role of the hired man but then, free of all chores, he would slip to the shores of the Peribonka. There he would linger along the high banks, alone in the solitude of the forest, his imagination quickened by the murmur of the river on its way to Lake St. John—and there, amid 'the birches, aspens, alders and wild cherries scattered on the slope,' he conceived the Chapdelaine story."

84
Dr Elizabeth Bagshaw (1881-1982)

Like most of the early feminists, Dr Bagshaw, who practised medicine in the slums of Hamilton and ran Canada's first birth-control clinic, was also an advocate of temperance. But although she would report to the authorities any narcotics abuse she observed in her daily rounds, she was far more lenient towards the liquor offences she encountered during the years when Ontario was enjoying prohibition. The reasons ranged from her understanding of the economic importance of booze in the ethnic communities to, it must be said, the vicarious thrill she received from being privy to the world of bootleggers. On one occasion an immigrant woman from Italy showed her a secret passage in her kitchen leading to the immense stockpile of illegal hooch. Another time she was whisked out of a patient's house to avoid being among the victims of a police raid. The person who urged her escape was Rocco Perri, who had known about the impending raid and already had removed his property. Perri, who was referred to in the press as the king of the bootleggers and was often implicated in gang wars, was a "nice fellow to meet, always gentlemanly, nice to talk to," Dr. Bagshaw recalled. She also pointed out that they shared a certain criminality. But whereas disseminating liquor became legal in 1927, disseminating birth-control information was against the law until 1969.

85
Lady Florence McCrea Eaton (1881-1970)

At the turn of the century, Florence McCrea, the daughter of a farm family from Omemee, Ontario, was training as a nurse in a private hospital in Toronto when John Craig (eventually Sir John) Eaton, head of the department store founded by his father, checked in as a patient. Romance flowered. "Jack joined me in Omemee and asked my father for his consent to our engagement [in March 1901] and marriage", she would remember. "Father had no thought of withholding his approval but he did ask, half seriously but half in fun, 'Why did you need to come to Omemee to find a wife?' Later, the two of us alone, Father told me he rather feared an easy life in luxury would not be good for me, as it was foreign to what I had known." She also recalled that other "girls of my own age or younger... wondered openly if there was a 'Jack *Simpson*' in Toronto too!"

86
A.Y. Jackson (1882-1974)

With Jackson as with other members of the Group of Seven if not perhaps with artists generally, reputation lagged behind notoriety by one full generation. Thus it was only at the end of the Second World War, after twenty years of widespread exhibiting, that Jackson began to earn a substantial income. In the 1950s, O.J. Firestone, an economist who would amass a collection of nearly seven hundred works by the Group, began hearing rumours that Jackson was involved actively in the stock market. Speculation seemed to have become almost a sideline for Jackson, going beyond the question of tips that mining promoters would sometimes give him on his sketching trips in the North. Firestone repeatedly tried to draw Jackson into conversation on the subject, only to learn that his interlocutor did not seem to care about the "basics of investment economics, including the principle of maximizing returns from alternate investment opportunities." While listening to what was said about the need to acquire expertise or cultivate experts, Jackson continued to go his own way, issuing buy orders and sell orders, quite out of character with what otherwise was his cautious disposition. The fact that he allowed incoming cheques to accumulate and go stale and sometimes hid cash in books and forgot about it—those traits were more in keeping with the collecting public's ideas of how an artist should behave.

87
Wyndham Lewis (1882-1957)

The painter, novelist and polemicist was born in Canada (aboard his father's yacht in the Bay of Fundy) and served as a Canadian war artist in the First World War. During the Second World War, the same trick of nationality allowed him to remain in Canada, where he endured considerable poverty while earning the emnity of the few people who tried to help him.

When Lewis was living in Windsor, for example, he sought the services of Paul Martin, the politician, in collecting a payment he was owed for a painting. Lewis suggested that he undertake a portrait of Mrs Nell Martin in lieu of legal fees, and her husband agreed. The painter and the sitter quarreled, however, particularly over the former's extreme right-wing political views and vitriolic denunciations of Canada and its inhabitants. Martin recalls him as "a very odd fellow, coming to the house every day but keeping on his galoshes, overcoat and hat while he sketched."

Martin, who didn't care for the completed picture, was unaware that in his absence Mrs Martin had agreed to renegotiate the fee to the advantage of Lewis—who then demanded another increase, without which he refused to sign the painting.

In the fullness of time, Martin has written, "the portrait has grown on me...It is still unsigned."

88
E.J. Pratt (1882-1964)

The Newfoundland poet, author of *The Titanic, Brébeuf and His Brethren* and other long narrative poems, had a cottage near Bobcaygeon, Ontario, to which he would retreat each summer after classes ended at the University of Toronto, where he taught. Before closing up the place one season and returning to the city, he contracted with a local builder to make a private "dock" on the property. He had used the term as it was used in Newfoundland, to mean a small enclosed dock, suitable for a child to swim in. When he returned the following summer, however, he found a "dock" in the mainland Canadian sense: a pier or wharf "big enough to moor a Kawartha Lakes steamer—and with a price to match." Thus was it brought home once again that Newfoundland and Canada are separated by a common language, that English Canada and French Canada plus Newfoundland equal two and one-half solitudes.

89
Louis St. Laurent (1882-1973)

St. Laurent's nickname "Uncle Louis" came to him only after he had been prime minister for five months. It was the coinage of a Tory journalist in the West who remarked during the 1949 general election campaign, "Uncle Louis is going to be hard to beat." What was intended as a derogatory reference was taken up as a term of endearment, one his staff made easy use of, as though to disguise their leader's stiff and awkward manner. At length, however, the sobriquet, and the new image based on it, began to affect the reality; the leader lost his rough edges, and the folksy charm of which he was rumoured capable soon existed in actuality.

90
Marius Barbeau (1883-1969)

John E. Robbins, diplomat and university president, on the pioneer folklorist:

"I remember that great spirit, Marius Barbeau, concluding a very heated discussion among French and English Canadians about 15 years ago at the Chateau Laurier, where everyone was at daggers drawn, remarking that the solution was so simple: love and the marriage bed. Then he read a charming quatrain which he'd made up on the spot while all the verbal missiles were flying. Then the meeting broke into laughter, and adjourned with people looking at each other as if they were human beings again."

91
Izaak Walton Killam (1885-1955)

Killam was a Montreal tycoon whose various business interests, especially in securities brokerage and later pulp and paper, are thought to have made him, for a time, Canada's richest man. "Killam had no flaws", one of his friends remembered. "He was just odd". Some of his eccentricities were active ones, such as marrying an American or leaving money to help set up the Canada Council even though his own love of culture was confined to detective stories. Certain other of his peculiarities were passive. He was known to stand at the window of his office for hours, contemplating the St Lawrence in silence, rousing himself only to scribble an occasional note. He attended parties but sat alone and without speaking, though on one such occasion he is reported to have said suddenly "My God, I need a million dollars" before getting to his feet and leaving. A young prehensile member of the St James's Club once found himself sharing a urinal with the great man. He remembered hearing that Killam had just returned from a southern holiday but couldn't recall the details. He said he hoped that the weather had been good in Barbados, but Killam didn't reply. He said he trusted that Killam had found Bermuda pleasant. Still no answer. As Killam left the lavatory he uttered one word and let it float back over his shoulder. "Nassau", he said, and was gone.

92

C.D. Howe (1886-1960)

The political career of the man who had been Mackenzie King's Minister of Everything ended with a thundering report in 1957 when he and so many other Liberals were driven from public life by John

Diefenbaker's victory in the general election. So as not to be subtle, Diefenbaker promptly prohibited the government from doing business with the engineering firm Howe had been associated with—twenty-two years earlier. Corporations did not offer him directorships because they feared losing their easy access to Ottawa.

The perhaps not entirely guileless exception was E.P. Taylor, who asked Howe to sit on the board of Domtar, the pulp and paper company he controlled. Then came an invitation from Lord Beaverbrook to join the board of another paper company, Price Brothers, which had recently been the target of a failed takeover attempt by Taylor. Visualising himself in a conflict of interest, and as the rope in a tug-of-war between two such financiers, Howe tried to withdraw gracefully, confiding to Beaverbook that "Eddie is sentimental, and to quarrel with him might be expensive". But neither tycoon would retract his hospitality. So Howe joined both organisations.

Beaverbrook thought Howe's presence would keep the Taylor forces at bay, but Howe increased his own interest in Price Brothers until he himself emerged as chairman. Beaverbrook then sought to appoint K.C. Irving to the board as another warning to Taylor. When Howe resisted, Beaverbrook threatened to look elsewhere for newsprint on which to publish his English newspapers. Howe was not lightly threatened nor easily outsmarted, however, and he promptly merged Price Brothers with a paper company controlled by Lord Rothermere, one of Beaverbrook's rivals in Fleet Street.

93
Vincent Starrett (1886-1973)

Starrett, the man-of-letters and mystery writer, the author of books such as *Murder on B Deck* and *The Private Life of Sherlock Holmes*, was born in Toronto, in a flat above the Upper Canada Bible and Tract Society bookshop, which his grandfather managed. The delivery was beset with complications. To those attending, it appeared that the baby had been born dead and that the mother might not survive. As a temporary measure, the infant was wrapped in a newspaper and placed under the bed until the body could be disposed of properly. The newspaper was *The Globe*. "Can any of my colleagues of the typewriter", Starrett would ask in later years, "point to an earlier appearance in print?"

94
Vincent Massey (1887-1967)

In 1952 it was announced that Vincent Massey—at various times Canadian ambassador to the United States, high commissioner to the Court of St James's, statesman, royal commissioner, author, arts patron and all-around public man—would be the governor-general. There was concern in certain circles that even so distinguished a native Canadian would diminish an office previously occupied exclusively by British noblemen, though the fears proved groundless. Indeed it was Lord Cranborne, lord privy seal in the Churchill government, who remarked of Massey, "Fine chap, Vincent, but he does make one feel a bit of a savage." At the other extreme were Canadians worried that Massey was in fact too patrician for the role (hence B.K. Sandwell's verse on the occasion about "the Masseys and the masses").

What neither faction could have imagined was the scene unfolding in Massey's bedchamber on the day of the investiture. Lady Tweedsmuir, the widow of a previous governor-general, had given Massey her husband's old uniform, noting that the two men were the same size and build. In not one of his many previous lives had Massey faced the problem of wearing such a rig, one that had been designed by the Prince Consort and included a plumed hat, tight trousers with stirrups, half-wellingtons, goose-neck spurs and various pieces of tack having to do with a ceremonial sword. It was necessary to don the components in a certain sequence if one were to emerge fully dressed. Massey was at the risk of missing the ceremony as he and his valet ran through various combinations. He was rescued by his brother Raymond, the Hollywood actor, who quickly and expertly took charge. For as it happened the film producer David O. Selznick had given Raymond an almost identical uniform to wear in *The Prisoner of Zenda* (1937).

95
General Andrew McNaughton (1887-1966)

"Usually, after we had finished our business, he would manage to turn the conversation to other subjects before I got up to take my leave", recalled one Canadian officer who had occasion to call on the Canadian commander every week early in the Second World War. "Once, I remember, we talked about beaver meadows in Canada—how did we get on that subject?—about which the General knew everything and I knew practically nothing. Another time he told me about the conversation he had had with Eisenhower in London the previous day. Another time he told me of how he had been summoned to see Churchill and of how, on being ushered in, he 'found Winston in his birthday suit.' Often he talked to me about weapon development and artillery practice as though I were as knowledgeable as he was in these matters. I might have difficulty in keeping up with him, I usually did, but it helped to send me away encouraged and refreshed."

96
Grey Owl (1888-1938)

Following his death, it became clear that the renowned Indian author and naturalist was in fact an Englishman named Archibald Stansfeld Belaney who had no native blood whatever. The deception had come about gradually and only got out of hand as late as 1931, when he was asked to address a convention in Montreal.

"The following morning [their friend] Sir Charles [Delme Radcliff] came, carrying a newspaper", according to Grey Owl's wife, Anahareo. "It was obvious that he was greatly agitated. Then, showing us the front-page picture of Archie and me that had been taken after the lecture, Sir Charles whacked the paper with the back of his hand and said, 'Just look at Anahareo—isn't it ghastly!' Since I had a cold at the time, my face looked like a boxing-glove. Then he pointed to the heading across the page. It read, in box-car letters: FULL-BLOODED INDIAN GIVES LECTURE ON WILDLIFE.

"'And what are you going to do about that?' asked Sir Charles, pointing to the headline.

"Archie said 'Why nothing, why spoil their little story?'

"Had Archie known how seriously people were going to take his ancestry, this would have been the time to have clamped down on that 'full-blooded Indian' stuff. But how was he to know that the more he wrote, the more Indian he became in the eyes of the public?"

97
Georges Vanier (1888-1967)

The diplomatist and statesman George Ignatieff was on the staff of Canada House in London when Mackenzie King paid a state visit in 1941. Accompanying King was his military adviser, Georges Vanier, the future governor-general. "He had lost a leg in World War I, and though he managed remarkably well with an artificial leg, he always carried a spare in case of trouble. 'Would you mind finding my spare leg?' he said to me as he left the plane. He was followed by Norman Robertson, the undersecretary of state for external affairs. When I asked Norman where I might find the general's leg, he replied that I was shouting in his deaf ear and he couldn't tell what I was saying. Jack Pickersgill, the prime minister's executive assistant and the fourth member of the official party, turned out to be deaf in the other ear and couldn't hear me either. It occurred to me that this strange delegation was not likely to add anything other than confusion to ar- already confused war effort."

98
General Morris (Two-Gun) Cohen (1889-1970)

The turning point in the life of Canada's most notorious soldier of fortune came in about 1908 in Saskatoon, where he was a professional gambler. One evening he was alone in a Chinese restaurant with the elderly proprietor, a man known as Mah Sam, when a third person entered and demanded the owner's cash and jewelry. "I saw it was a hold-up, but I wasn't heeled—that is, armed—and I had to be careful", Cohen would recall many years later. "I closed in till I was too near for him to use his rod and socked him on the jaw."

He then retrieved the booty and waited for the thief to regain consciousness, whereupon he "gave him a kick in the pants—maybe two kicks—and told him to beat it."

So began the close friendship between Mah Sam and Cohen. As it happened, the former was the local representative of the revolutionary movement dedicated to overthrowing the Manchu dynasty in China, and Cohen became the conduit between the rebels and the English-speaking community in western Canada. He was introduced to Dr Sun Yat-Sen during one of Sun's speaking tours and later invited to China as one of his bodyguards. He was made a general in the Chinese army following Sun's death in 1922, and for most of the next four decades worked in China as a freelance military adviser, arms dealer and jack of all trades, maintaining good relations with both Beijing and Taipai following the 1949 revolution. He was Canada's *other* gift to China: the reverse of the coin whose obverse was Dr Norman Bethune.

99

Frank Underhill (1889-1971)

In 1914, the historian and social critic took up his first teaching post, at the still-new University of Saskatchewan. Compared to Oxford, whence he'd come, he found Saskatoon a depressing spot. "As far as one can judge this place is even worse for church-going than Toronto or Edinburgh", he informed his mother, predicting that he would soon be reduced to attending Sunday services, or even motion pictures, simply for something to do. "But I shall ward off the day when I start as long as possible." Little time had passed, however, before he was not only a church- and cinema-goer but a patron of wrestling matches.

100
Dr Norman Bethune (1890-1939)

Even the most casual look at Bethune's life shows his psychological complexity. On one occasion as a young general practitioner in rural Ontario, he treated a bedridden patient and then did the necessary chores around the man's farm. That side of his nature found mature expression in the noble work he performed in field hospitals during the Spanish Civil War and the Chinese Revolution. But there was always another aspect to Bethune's personality — volatile, aggressive and destructive. One of the most bizarre illustrations came in 1927 when his wife, who had separated from him and was seeking a divorce at the time, reported that she had been mistreated by a male friend, a successful American businessman. Bethune, who feared that the tuberculosis from which he was suffering might prove fatal, resolved to call the blackguard out, murder him, and then surrender to the police. Accordingly, he went to Pittsburgh, lured the man to a hotel room, and threatened him with a pistol. When the victim confessed his guilt and begged to be shot, Bethune softened his intentions but using the gun as a club dealt the man severe blows to the face and head. He then treated the wounds, shared a bottle of liquor with his antagonist, and helped spirit him away from the hotel unseen. Bethune kept a blood-stained hotel towel as a souvenir.

101
Maurice Duplessis (1890-1959)

The Quebec premier was frequently less rigid in private than he usually appeared publicly. One historian has illustrated the point by describing an occasion in 1938 when Duplessis invited three members of the Royal Commission on Dominion-Provincial Relations to stop by his office for a drink—Joseph Sirois, a law professor; J.W. Dafoe, the editor of the Winnipeg *Free Press*; and Louis St. Laurent. They were plied with much champagne and then asked to be the premier's guests for dinner at eight p.m. at the Chateau Frontenac. Duplessis, unsteady on his legs, arrived late, only to deride the others, who had been waiting forty-five minutes, for their tardiness. He then ridiculed Dafoe through dinner to the extent that Sirois and St. Laurent began to feel embarrassed as Quebeckers. After dinner, the guests of honour made good their escape while the celebrations continued in their absence, at a suite in the hotel. Cases of champagne were delivered; unsatisfactory ones were thrown out the fire door. China, stemware and other goods were flung about the room, with the premier proving himself adept at hurling champagne glasses at light fixtures. The party went on in all its boisterousness until early the following morning. By that time, one man had been hurt by flying glass. An aide to the premier led the victim down the fire escape and back into the hotel via the lobby, so that it would seem he had suffered an accident in the street.

102
Aimee Semple McPherson (1890-1944)

In the 1920s, Aimee Semple McPherson, the flamboyant founder of the Angelus Temple of the Four Square Gospel, in Los Angeles, was perhaps the world's best known hell-fire preacher, even before a series of romantic and financial scandals rocked her ministry.

Her religious life began in 1907 in Ingersoll, Ontario, her native town, when, as young Aimee Kennedy, she attended a revival meeting conducted by an itinerant evangelist. She was thrown into trance-like ecstasy by his sermonizing, and she later called on him to express her thanks and wonderment.

"Reverend ... pastor...." She faltered, uncertain how to address him.

"Robert Semple is all", he replied. "Come in. Come in!"

"The other night—." Again she hesitated.

"You were at the meeting. And praise God, He's spoken to your heart!"

"Yes. Yes!"

"And He's won your precious soul to Himself. So you've come to share your joy, for it's full to overflowing."

"How did you *know*?"

"Ah, the hunger was in your face that night. And the fullness and peace in there now, as I've seen it in a hundred others," he explained. "So praise God for you, my new sister in the Lord!"

So saying, he took her hands in his.

He soon became her first husband.

103
Sir Frederick Banting (1891-1941)

Once he shared in the Nobel Prize for medicine in 1923 for his co-discovery of insulin, Banting was heralded by magazines as the most famous living Canadian. He found such status a difficult burden. Art was one source of comfort, and he became a friend, disciple and painting companion of several members of the Group of Seven, particularly A.Y. Jackson. He grew to be a more than competent painter of that school but was never accepted as anything other than a poseur, to judge from a remark by Thoreau MacDonald, the illustrator. On the evidence of his letters, journals and reputation, MacDonald must rank as one of the most unmalicious, even-tempered figures in the whole history of Canadian art. Yet when

Banting was killed in an air crash in Newfoundland, MacDonald confided this to the painter Carl Schaefer: "Suppose you've heard of Banting's end, too bad, but at least he won't do any more painting."

104
Samuel Bronfman (1891?-1971)

The chairman of Seagrams, the world's largest liquor company, was an autocrat who disclosed as little corporate information as possible, presided over carefully scripted shareholders' meetings and feuded with family members. Yet according to the testimony of some people who knew him well, he endured crushing personal defeats, though not in Stoic silence for such was not his nature. He never hid his disappointment with successive governments for failing to recommend his appointment to the Senate, for example. Two other outstanding instances concern his touching affection for the Royal Family.

Bronfman had secured seats for himself and his family for the Coronation in Westminster Abbey in June 1953, but was horrified to learn that they were behind a pillar. One of his underlings located another guest who was prepared to give up his own seats so that the Bronfmans might enjoy a better view of the ceremony. Mr Sam, as he was known inside Seagrams (to distinguish him from his brother, Mr Allan), "accepted the ... kindness almost as a matter of right."

The same executive has recalled that Mr Sam's "swearing could frequently be heard ... in my office when he lambasted his brother on some matter or other... One evening when the swearing reached an all-time high, I crossed the mezzanine floor to see what was wrong. I had no sooner looked around the corner into Mr. Sam's office when a telephone, torn out of its wall socket, went sailing by my head to crash on the floor. I thought Mr. Sam had gone raving mad. His language was unbelievable." It seems that Mr. Allan, rather than Mr. Sam, had been invited to sit at the head table during a dinner in honour of the Queen Mother.

105
Tim Buck (1891-1973)

Buck was one of the founders of the Communist Party of Canada and served as its general secretary for thirty-two years. Frederick Griffin of the Toronto *Daily Star* described the scene when Buck and eight other party leaders were sent to prison in 1931 for belonging to a forbidden organisation.

"They sat in the row of seats ... until the judge, sharply, told them to stand up. They stood in line, without plea or fear, without mockery and without rebellion. Certainly in this drama of Canadian justice these Communists did not, by word or deed, detract from its dignity.

"Thus standing, they met their punishment.

"For them there was no procession of clergymen, no neighbours, no comrades, no score or more of character witnesses to say that they were good citizens, churchgoers, kind fathers, philanthropists, honest men who had never taken an unearned nickel, honourable men who had never broken their word. Their character was not in question, merely their ideas and ideals. For them their single lawyer spoke but briefly. A few words, and he was done.

"The judge invited them to speak. The small Tim Buck alone responded. He did not beg; he did not plead; he took a pace forward like a soldier and, looking front, said, 'I accept the sentence of the court. I only hope that those who trusted me will find that I proved worthy.'

"Then he stepped back...

"The court was silent when Mr. Justice Wright pronounced sentence that sent these men to Kingston Penitentiary for terms up to five years. A full-voiced man, he spoke quietly, as if he felt that the occasion was historic, the outlawing of Communism as a philosophy and force in Canada...

"The condemned men stepped out smartly as a file of soldiers. Only a wave of Buck's hand, a short smile of farewell to a friend, showed that they were really men and not ideas who were going to jail."

106
Nathan Phillips (1892-1976)

When the perennial Toronto politician ("Mayor of All the People") was an adolescent in Cornwall, Ontario, he sometimes relieved classroom boredom by "secretly scribbling my name and adding progressively the various titles I hoped to add." Thus in his imagination he became Nathan Phillips, Barrister and Solicitor, K.C. —all of which he would achieve in real life. Then he would append the initials MP. "Not content I prefixed the word 'Hon.' to indicate Cabinet rank, and I stuck the word 'Right' before 'Hon.' thereby making me a Privy Councillor. Having got that far I saw no reason why I shouldn't be Prime Minister and for good measure I conferred a Knighthood on myself."

107
Mary Pickford (1893-1979)

Ethel Clegg, an older child in the neighbourhood, recalled entering the Smith house in downtown Toronto to discover her sometime playmate, Gladys Smith, the future Mary Pickford, pinching her cheeks and sticking herself repeatedly with a hairpin. "I'm trying to make my cheeks red like Nellie Marshall's", she explained. Nellie Marshall was a popular local actress. The year was 1898; Gladys Smith was only five.

108
Billy Bishop (1894-1956)

A fellow First World War flier described Canada's (and the Empire's) greatest flying ace as "a fantastic shot but a terrible pilot". Two anecdotes suggest that the same characterization might apply to his aerobatics on the social circuit. On leave in London, he found himself in demand as a luncheon companion of the attorney general and dinner guest of Lord Beaverbrook. But in order to spend time with a young actress he had met earlier in the day at the Savoy, he ducked another invitation, an evening with Bonar Law, the Canadian who was then chancellor of the Exchequer and would soon be PM. His mentor and patron Lady St. Helier learned of the episode and was caustic. Not only should a gentleman keep appointments with his betters, she chided him, he must also ensure that his hairbrushes are clean at all times. "I found yours in the bathroom in disgraceful condition", she pointed out.

Later, between the wars, Bishop was in Berlin and met socially with the Nazi deputy Hermann Goering, himself a much-decorated fighter pilot in the 1914-18 conflict.

"I've been curious to know what you called us", Bishop said to his once and future adversary. "We always referred to you as Huns because it was the worst thing we could think of."

"Oh, we just called you Britishers", Goering replied. "We always considered that quite bad enough."

Harold Innis (1894-1952)

Many have attested to the obvious importance of Innis's work in political economy, especially his "staple thesis" and his perceptions of the function of the mass media. Some also have noted the convoluted prose in which such ideas were expressed. For example, the military historian C.P. Stacey has written, "The late Harold Innis, so much admired, was a supposed expert on communications who was quite unable to communicate." But much less attention has been paid to Innis's crude yet effective style in academic politics. When in 1929 he was passed over for promotion at the University of Toronto, he resigned angrily, causing the university to change its mind and make him an associate professor after all: if not the first then certainly the last time such a tactic ever worked to an umbrage-taker's satisfaction. Ten years later he quit the Royal Society of Canada when a book he considered unworthy received its medal for literature. The criteria for future recipients were then changed so that Innis might rejoin. Innis grew weary of academic democracy, saying, "Discussion has become a menace rather than a solvent to the problems of a complex society." So he was a natural foe of Frank Underhill, the always liberal and sometimes socialist historian and commentator. Yet in 1941, when Underhill prophesied and lamented that waning British influence in Canada must inevitably be paid for by an even stronger US presence, Innis defended him against calls for his resignation. He agreed with Underhill's assessment; in fact, he saw it as a far blacker prospect than Underhill. Morever, Innis could appreciate the narrow issue involved—the sanctity of the tenure system.

Roy Thomson, 1st Baron Thomson of Fleet (1894-1976)

The diplomat Charles Ritchie noted in his diary a lunch in 1969 "with a group of super-rich oil men at the Dorchester, organized by Roy Thomson, who said it did him good to hear talk which seldom got below the level of a billion dollars. I found the conversation fascinating, though sometimes incomprehensible. Plainly I had been invited as a social or symbolic gesture—I came with the flowers, the smoked salmon, and the wine, to show that the old pirate knew the amenities."

111

John Diefenbaker (1895-1979)

Diefenbaker's eminent legal career, which extended over thirty-six years until he became leader of the Progressive Conservative Party, began inauspiciously in 1919 in Wakaw, Saskatchewan, population six hundred. The residents "were particularly litigious, in a court at a moment's notice", but they did not welcome an outsider at first. Diefenbaker had difficulty finding office space or even a place to sleep, much less citizens dissatisfied with the town's other solicitor, who was well liked and long established. In fact Diefenbaker's first client was his brother Elmer who paid him one dollar, remarking as he did so that fraternal affection was causing him to fork over more than the advice he received was worth. His fortunes seemed to improve when he was hired to defend a farmer accused of wounding his neighbour with a shotgun and the jury returned a verdict of innocent, though later it became known that more luck than skill was involved. A juror revealed that it had been decided to encourage the lawyer in his first case by finding the accused guilty of a lesser charge. When someone reported that it was Diefenbaker's birthday, the jury decided on acquittal instead. Thus Diefenbaker's practice was established, and he was soon busy with his share of the community's arson cases. These were so numerous that his office burned down twice when suspicious fires spread out of control.

112
Red Ryan (1896-1935)

Ryan was perhaps the most infamous Canadian criminal of the 1920s and 1930s, a flamboyant bank robber, cracksman and murderer. In 1923 he escaped from Kingston Penitentiary but was recaptured three months later. He claimed to have changed his ways, and used his notoriety to dissuade young people from following in his path. A public campaign, initiated by a Roman Catholic priest, Fr W.T. Kingsley, finally brought him parole, and he was held up as proof that prison can rehabilitate. Ryan then led a double life—by day an anti-crime crusader, by night a criminal.

"One night at a Kingston dinner party, a guest, gazing intently at Ryan's hair, remarked that it was not its usual light red but oddly dark in places", the journalist Roy Greenaway wrote years later. "Ryan was noticeably embarrassed at this, and gave voice to his displeasure." It seems that he was the tall dark-haired man who, according to press reports, had been seen leading a gang of bank robbers.

But only eight months after his release, the jig (as Ryan might have said) was up. He was shot and killed by police while robbing a liquor store in Sarnia, Ontario.

Greenaway called on Fr Kingsley and found him tearing up a photo inscribed "To my very loyal friend, Rev. W.T. Kingsley, from

Norman 'Red' Ryan." In a short time the priest suffered a stroke, and died soon afterward.

In the period following his parole "Ryan was responsible for killing two men and making a third an invalid", Greenaway wrote. "In my books, Ryan killed another man ..just the same as if he had fired the gun at his benefactor's head." He meant Fr Kingsley of the Church of the Good Thief.

113
Sir William Stephenson (1896-   )

In January 1901, the future spy-master, who would become known in the popular press by the code-name Intrepid, saw the streets of Winnipeg draped in black, owing to the recent death of Queen Victoria. The five-year-old mistook the sight as mourning for his father, who had been killed in the South African war a few weeks earlier.

114
Lester Pearson (1897-1972)

In January 1965, Pearson was to meet with President Lyndon Johnson at the latter's Texas ranch to sign the Auto Pact. The External Affairs minister, Paul Martin, and the ambassador to Washington, Charles Ritchie, flew in first and were met on the tarmac by the president and Lady Bird Johnson, the first lady, and whisked away by jeep, with the chief executive at the wheel, for a tour of the property. When they had driven furiously for a half hour (without leaving the Johnson spread), the telephone rang announcing the arrival of Pearson's aircraft. The president drove to the podium prepared for the occasion and, making a grand display for the television cameras, welcomed his friend Drew Pearson, the Canadian prime minister. In his own account of the incident, however, Pearson stated that the president had greeted him as Harold Wilson. Martin speculates that Pearson misremembered the wording because he found it "less embarrassing...to be confused with the British prime minister than with the well-known Washington journalist."

115

Floyd S. Chalmers (1898-   )

In 1946, the magazine publisher and arts patron attended a meeting of Commonwealth news executives in London, where the pall of wartime austerity had not yet begun to lift. The delegates were received at Buckingham Palace by King George and Queen Elizabeth. The King complained of a chill in the palace and one of the guests, the editor of a British Columbia weekly, shattered protocol by offering to send one of the thick pullovers made by the Siwash Indians of his home province. The King accepted with alacrity. With the precedent thus established, Chalmers thought he should offer a gift as well. But, as he confessed to the Queen's private secretary, he possessed nothing that was desirable except for a couple of dozen pairs of nylon stockings, which were extremely difficult to come by in Canada and virtually priceless in Britain. The official replied that the Queen had of course heard of such garments but did not possess any and would "give anything for a couple of pairs." Chalmers promised to deliver some but could not bring himself to do so. "I could not convince myself that it was fitting for me to send nylon stockings to Her Britannic Majesty", he wrote.

116
John Neville (1898?-1963?)

Neville, aka Lord Neville, aka Edward Montague, was a self-educated Toronto stockbroker who became Canada's most successful and most sophisticated swindler. He used bluff and personal charm to extort millions of dollars from Canadians, Americans and Britons—everyone from indigent widows to show business figures and peers of the realm—using a variation of the Ponzi scheme or pyramid. At length he was sent to prison in the US, then deported to his native country. "I vowed to myself in prison that if I ever got my hand on a dollar again, I'd squeeze it till it was dry", he said on his return to a Toronto journalist who covered Neville's doings off and on for fifteen years. "I've proved that I can. All I bought in Windsor this morning was a ten-cent pocket comb and this." He pointed to a secondhand copy of Cicero. Already a master of modern languages, he had taught himself Latin behind bars.

Two years later he was back in business.

117
Helen Creighton (1899-   )

One of Canada's best known folklorists and collectors of folk songs was a Dartmouth teenager, asleep in her bed, when the munitions ship *Mount Blanc* collided with another vessel on December 6, 1917, causing the loudest manmade noise ever heard up to that time: the Great Halifax Explosion, in which fifteen hundred people were killed and six thousand injured. With a girlfriend, she hastened to find her father who had crossed the harbour to Halifax only a short time before. "We dressed hastily, shaking tiny fragments of glass from our shoes for it had penetrated everywhere. Then we ran to the ferry.

Dartmouth ferries have a remarkable record and not even this calamity stopped them although blood and broken glass were everywhere."

Once she determined that her father was safe, Creighton "got the car out and started downtown to offer help wherever needed, but there was so much glass on the street that in no time I had a flat tire" and so three citizens had to come to aid her instead. That problem solved, she spent the next several days as a volunteer, helping where possible with medical and housing problems.

Not long afterwards, a man approached her as she waited for the ferry "with a sheet of paper in his hand with a song on it about the explosion. He wanted to sell it to us. I took one look and saw a line which read, 'There lies a little baby's hand and there an old man's head.' I gave it back in a hurry and we laughed at anything so gruesome. Little did I know the time would come when I would scour the land for someone with a song of the explosion. I found one in 1933 and another twenty years later, but I have never come across that ballad sheet, or indeed any other."

118
Charles Feinberg (1899-1988)

Feinberg left school in Peterborough, Ontario, at age twelve to work as a messenger and wallpaper salesman for $2.50 per week. Of that sum, two dollars went to help support the household; much of the remaining fifty cents found its way to a local secondhand store that featured a generous supply of used books. "They would sell you a book for a nickel", he would recall. "The lovely thing was, you could bring back the book, and they'd give you three cents' credit. There was no law that said that you had to eat lunch every day; so you ate an apple or a banana and bought a book." One day, however, he was offered a book for ten cents instead of five. "Here, boy," said the shop keeper, "buy this book and see if you like it—bring it back if you don't." The book was *American Poems* edited by William Michael Rossetti (1872) containing some poems by Walt Whitman, to whom the anthology was dedicated. Feinberg's curiosity was aroused. By 1916 he had purchased his first Whitman manuscript, a letter, for $7.50. In time, financed by the petroleum fortune he amassed in the United States, Feinberg would own half of the two thousand or so extant Whitman letters as well as sixteen hundred of the equal number of surviving letters sent *to* Whitman. Together with printed books, photographs and the like, they would form one of the most extraordinary, extensive, famous and valuable collections of a single author ever assembled, one that has virtually made Whitman scholarship possible.

119
K.C. Irving (1899-)

The New Brunswick industrialist showed his colours even as a young boy. "When the noise of the pet ducks he was raising in the family yard brought complaints from the neighbours, he had the ducks killed and sold them to the complainants, thereby solving the diplomatic problem and netting himself $100 besides."

120
F.R. Scott (1899-1985)

The civil libertarian, poet and expert on constitutional law was the product of a large and distinguished family. His father, for example, was Frederick George Scott, a radical Anglican priest and minor poet. In 1916, Rev Scott was serving as a military chaplain in France when he learned that another of his sons, Harry, had been killed in action and his body hastily interred on the battlefield. In order that he might conduct a proper burial service over the remains, he led a frantic twenty-four-hour search for the grave. The first one he dug up proved empty. But in the second he soon came upon "darling Harry's left hand with the signet ring on his little finger." He described the mission to the other members of the family in an anguished eleven-page letter. The act of reading it, the teenaged Frank, a student at Bishop's College, confided to his diary, "made me feel proud to belong to a family like ours, and made me want to live up to our standard. 'To be a good Scott one must live without spot,' I think ought to be our motto."

121
Roland Michener (1900-   )

In 1969, Governor-General Michener was presenting the annual Governor-General's Literary Awards in a ceremony at Rideau Hall. As an aide called out each winner's name and city of residence, the writer would step forward to receive the prize. When Mordecai Richler's turn came, the vice-regent, perhaps after registering no more than the word "Montreal", began speaking to Richler in French.

"*Êtes-vous canadien?*" he asked.

Richler was startled but managed to reply, "*Oui.*"

Michener rattled on for a moment in further French. When he seemed to be done, Richler said "*Merci*" and resumed his seat.

"I did not correct the Governor-General", he reported later, because he felt it was his turn to illustrate *noblesse oblige.*

122
Gordon Sinclair (1900-84)

In the 1920s and 1930s, many colourful and indeed often pre-posterous newspaper reporters were popular heroes if not actual public figures. Sinclair was one of the most outstanding examples. In twenty-one years' full-time work with the Toronto *Star* plus various special appearances, he covered Chicago gangsters and the Dionne quintuplets, interviewed Hitler and Gandhi, made five sensation-gathering trips around the world ("LEECHES LIKE HOTDOGS FEED ON SINCLAIR'S BLOOD") and was fired eleven times. He then began a career in broadcasting that lasted twice as long.

The switch to radio came in 1942. Sinclair was too old to join the armed forces, had been refused credentials as a war correspondent, and was feuding with the *Star*. An acquaintance in radio telephoned to ask a favour. The station had received discs from a US correspondent describing the disastrous raid on Dieppe by the South Saskatchewan Regiment and others. Unfortunately the American had mispronounced Saskatchewan throughout. Could Sinclair help? In twenty minutes he wrote a commentary to be used in place of the recordings and the following day another, and so on. That was in August. No one at the newspaper noticed the regular daily broadcasts until February, when he received a memo from management asking how much he was being paid. "None of your damned business" was his scribbled reply. This time the firing took root.

123
Joey Smallwood (1900-   )

In 1968, Pierre Trudeau, visiting Newfoundland, had an audience with Premier Smallwood, who pledged his continued support of the federal Liberals but soon got off the conversational track.

"Do you ever cry, Mr. Trudeau?" he asked. For once Trudeau was at a loss for words. "You know, I cry every day!" Smallwood volunteered.

The premier then instructed his assembled ministers to say something in French to prove how well they could speak the language when the situation arose. He then announced that he was enjoying James A. Michener's novel *The Source*. He asked all members of the cabinet in turn whether they had read it. None had. He ordered them to do so within the next forty-eight hours.

124
James Bannerman (1902-70)

The pioneer Canadian broadcaster, actor and radio-dramatist, whose real name was John Charles Kirkpatrick McNaught, was well loved in life and sorely missed in death. "He never spoke meanly about anyone", according to a colleague. "Indeed, if he had a fault, it was in his somewhat overpowering habit of praising people to their faces. Once, when he was too drunk to drive back from a conference at Kingston, I took the wheel of his Sunbeam Talbot. After we had gone a few miles, he roused himself to say, 'She loves the feel of your hand on the wheel; she knows there's a master driving her.' It was enough to make the gorge rise, but it was typical Bannerman."

125
Donald Creighton (1902-79)

There was another, less dour side to Canada's most redoubtable narrative historian, the reserved and severe-looking figure who is known for his biography of Sir John A. Macdonald and other works.

"As did a number of other distinguished writers, Donald had spent 'that summer'—1928—in Paris", a friend recalled. "Accompanied by his recent bride Luella, and intent on historical research, he did not, like John Glassco, pursue outre amours, or, like Morley Callaghan, box with Hemingway, but he could give comparable vivid descriptions of aspects of his life there, such as a wonderful evocation of the atmosphere at the Bibliothèque Nationale, where he was doing his research, which, on hot days, became fetid and required the services of a man with a deodorant spray gun. Better still was his recollection of the performances of the great Paris music hall artists. He could sing verse after verse of their songs, and to have Mistinguett or Chevalier recreated out of Donald's rather gothic demeanor at luncheon in Brooklin [Ontario], was a startling pleasure."

126
Morley Callaghan (1903-   )

"Morley Callaghan's general knowledge is wide," said one of the novelist's colleagues on a CBC Radio quiz programme of the 1950s, "but it rarely came out in our broadcasts. His role seemed to be that of the argumentative bystander, who could whip up a storm of outrage about anything. The only piece of music I ever heard him refer to, and which he would quote at any opportunity, was *I'm*

Captain Jinks of the Horse Marines; I feed my horse on pork and beans. He used to complain that there were so few questions about sport..."

127
Paul Martin (1903-   )

"Shortly after our wedding [in 1937], Mackenzie King invited Nell and me to a dinner he was hosting for three recently married Liberal members", the long-serving cabinet minister recalls. "It was the first time I had visited Laurier House as a guest of the prime minister, and I was a little nervous. Coaching Nell a bit beforehand, I explained that this man was my boss and that much of my career would depend on him. Nell told me not to worry. When we arrived at the door, the prime minister laid on all his charm for her. 'How do you do, Mr. Prime Minister?' began Nell. 'My husband thinks you're a very great man.' 'And what do you think, Mrs. Martin?' 'Well,' she said, 'I'm going to need some convincing.' I just about dropped from embarrassment and fidgeted for the rest of the meal. King seemed to take it in good form, though. At about four o'clock the next afternoon, there was a knock at the door of our little flat on Delaware Avenue. I was in the back of the apartment and heard Nell say, 'Hello, Mr. King.' It was the prime minister, who had been so taken with Nell that he had come to invite her out for an afternoon stroll. I did not dare make an appearance. When Nell returned, she quipped, 'Well, Paul, you're made now!' This was her sweet revenge for my fretting."

128
Thomas Raddall (1903-   )

When the historical novelist was named the winner of the 1943
Governor-General's Award for fiction for his book *The Pied Piper
of Dipper Creek,* he declined to attend the ceremony, being held
in Toronto that year, even after his publishers, McClelland &
Stewart, offered to pay half his fare from the Maritimes. Since the
establishment of the awards in 1936 it had been customary for those
attending to wear formal dress. Raddall thought the requirement too
undignified—that is to say, too dignified—for "working writers", and
someone had to accept the medal on his behalf. The erosion of standards was thus set in motion, and by the time of his next win in
1948 (for *Halifax: Warden of the North,* non-fiction) Raddall could
turn up in a jacket and white flannels and not be thought out of place.
He was again in the vanguard in his response to winning a third
GG, for *The Path of Destiny,* non-fiction, in 1957. When the presen-
tations were made he was out of the country, thus prefiguring those
in the 1960s and 1970s who, for political or promotional reasons,
could be depended upon to boycott the awards.

129
Phyllis Ross (1903-88)

During the Second World War, Phyllis Gregory Turner (as she was
then styled—before her later marriage to Frank Ross, the lieutenant-
governor of British Columbia), held an annual position in the
burgeoning federal bureaucracy. She was in charge of the alloca-
tion of various natural oils, such as might be used in the manufac-
ture of explosives. So it was that the Vancouver *Province* described
this intelligent and formidable woman, trained as an economist in

Canada, Britain and the US, as a "glamour girl of fats and oils".

"For several months, hip-booted and oilskinned, the glamorous young widow with the stamp of Bryn Mawr had toured the ports of the Maritimes persuading skeptical fishermen to save the codfish livers they had usually thrown away", writes the biographer of Donald Gordon, the future president of the Canadian National Railways who was then, as head of Wartime Prices and Trade Board, her boss.

Gordon met her for the first time after she had finished her assignment in the East and had gone to British Columbia, on a similar mission concerning dogfish oil.

"My God," said Gordon, "I didn't even know a dogfish had a liver."

She was at the time the highest-ranking female in the Canadian civil service, though she was paid a third less than her male counterparts.

One of her children, John Turner, would become prime minister.

130
Tommy Douglas (1904-86)

The swearing in of a new government, whether provincial or federal, is not only informed by protocol but is usually accompanied by at least the appearance of good will on the part of the one that is being supplanted. Outgoing ministers are customarily given whatever time they need to remove personal papers from their files and otherwise tidy up their affairs. In return, they are expected to be magnanimous in defeat. Not so, however, when Douglas led the CCF to victory over the Liberals in Saskatchewan in 1944, thereby ushering in Canada's, indeed North America's, first socialist government.

"From my experience in sports, I'd always taken for granted that you chat with the fellow who had lost on a friendly basis, but it wasn't easy in this case", Douglas was to recall. "I remember meeting Dr. [John Michael] Urich and saying, 'Have you any suggestions for a man taking over the Department of Public Health?'

"He said, 'You made the promises, you know all the answers—go ahead and see what you can do.'

"I said, 'That is precisely what we intend to do, Doctor. I'll just give you a tip that we plan to do more in the next four years than you've done in the last twenty-five.'"

Douglas had not been premier long when he was struck deathly ill during a train journey and had to be rushed to hospital. "I think the only thing that saved me was that just the week before, penicillin, which had been only on the military list, had been released by the army for civilian use." The drug was still an expensive one, however, and accounted for a large part of his hospital bill, which came to the figure, staggering at the time, of a thousand dollars. Douglas had to borrow the money. "This gives you some idea of why hospital insurance certainly appealed to me", he said.

131
Paul-Emile Borduas (1905-60)

In the 1950s, Borduas was visiting Toronto from his exile in Paris and was the guest of honour at a party given by A.Y. Jackson. The two painters had never met. On the face of it, Borduas, the leading member of *les automatistes* and the principal author of the surrealist manifesto *Refus global,* can have had little in common with Jackson. But he might have been expected at least to have known of Jackson's role in the Group of Seven or heard of his lifelong commitment to the bicultural nature of Canadian art. After they had chatted pleasantly in French for much of the evening, however, Borduas asked, "By the way, do you paint, Mr. Jackson?" In subsequent years Jackson told the story as a sad proof of how never the twain shall meet after all.

132
Walter Gordon (1906-87)

The future nationalist and Liberal cabinet minister began his professional life as an accounting student in the famous Toronto firm of Clarkson, Gordon, in which his father, H.D. Lockhart Gordon, was then associated with G.T. Clarkson. (So great was Clarkson's influence in the provincial government that, according to *Hush,* the scandal tabloid, he was known in Queen's Park by the nickname "Jesus Christ"; Clarkson's lawyer cautioned him against suing the paper for libel, however, pointing out that "the present state of religious feeling in this province [is such that] no jury would think your reputation has been damaged merely because you were compared" with Him).

In any event, the young Gordon was quickly made "a sort of glorified office boy" attached to a new client, the Royal Commission on Customs and Excise, which was touring western Canada, conducting hearings.

"The importance of my rather ill-defined responsibilities was brought home to me as the commission was approaching Winnipeg", Gordon would recall. One of the commissioners was an Ontario Supreme Court judge with "the ability to sleep soundly through much of the day but, at critical moments, without appearing to wake up, to ask extremely pertinent questions of the witnesses." The judge asked Gordon to determine the identity of the leading bootlegger in each city and secure two bottles of alleged scotch without arousing the suspicions of the former politician and abiding teetotaller who headed the commission. If unsure which bootlegger was the best, the judge told him, he could always consult the senior RCMP officer. "My recollection is that I was able to carry out this mission satisfactorily", he wrote. The rest is political history.

133
Andrew Allan (1907-74)

The virtual father of Canadian radio drama, honoured for his acting as well as his directing, got off to a somewhat wobbly start in show business. As an undergraduate at the University of Toronto in the late 1920s he was called on to understudy the role of Egeus in a Hart House production of *A Midsummer-Night's Dream.* In the all-important exchange at the beginning of the first scene, he managed to utter the opening line, "Happy be Theseus, our renowed duke!", eliciting from his interlocutor the expected line, "Thanks, good Egeus: what's the news with thee?"

"Full of vexation, come I, with complaint/ Against my child, my daughter Hermia", Allan replied. But the ensuing twenty-two lines eluded him, as did no doubt the remainder of the play. The silence, he remembered many years later, was as long as the one "described in the Apocalypse after the opening of the seventh seal."

Finally his companion on stage came to his rescue, saying, "My good Egeus, I know what thou wouldst say—." He then extemporised an abtract of the speech in passable Shakespearean diction.

Allan continued to act throughout his student days. The experience proved useful on one occasion, he recalled. After six weeks, rehearsals included, of *Antony and Cleopatra* he sat down to an important English literature examination to find essay questions on, yes, *Antony and Cleopatra.*

134
Hugh MacLennan (1907-   )

MacLennan was acclaimed an important Canadian writer following the appearance in 1941 of his first novel, *Barometer Rising,* which centred on the Halifax explosion of 1917: the largest and loudest man-made explosion in the world until the invention of the atomic bomb. Where had MacLennan himself been when the event took place? In the lavatory of the family home in South Park Street, Halifax. As he was leaving for school, his mother, Frances Mac-Lennan, noticed that his knees were not clean (this was in the age when schoolboys wore short pants rather than trousers) and sent him to scrub them. Upon hearing the deafening blast, she and the family's maid rushed with young Hugh to the cellar, where they fell to their (in his case, presumably still unwashed) knees in prayer. His father, a physician, was in his surgery preparing to operate on a patient. A year earlier, Dr MacLennan had blown up the family's home after striking a match to investigate the source of a gas leak.

135
Florence Bird (1908-   )

Bird, the journalist and broadcaster who was selected in 1967 to head the Royal Commission on the Status of Women, first became aware of the special problems of working-class women through contact with a succession of cleaning ladies. One incident, in Montreal in the 1930s, left a particularly vivid impression on her. The eldest child of Bird's char required immediate brain surgery after being struck by an automobile. By law, the operation couldn't proceed unless the child's father gave his approval. His consent was secured in the nick of time only after police made a systematic search of cinemas and taverns. Had the man not been located, the child would have died, a victim of the fact that the wife and mother couldn't authorize what needed to be done. Indeed, under the civil code that obtained in Quebec until the 1960s, married women, like minors, convicts and imbeciles, were forbidden to enter into contracts. "I decided that laws as well as the attitude of society needed to be changed", Bird recalled. Her appointment by Lester Pearson came after she had crusaded for women's rights for several decades, using the pseudonym Anne Francis.

136
John Kenneth Galbraith (1908-   )

In his memoirs, the famous liberal economist recalls an occasion when his former Canadian citizenship proved useful in the pursuit of diplomacy. For ten years or more, the governments of the United States and Canada, on behalf of their respective airline lobbies, had been engaged in a fruitless wrangle over the question of reciprocal landing rights. To resolve the deadlock, it was suggested, a special two-person committee might be struck. President John F. Kennedy appointed Galbraith, who had recently returned from the post of US ambassador to India, to be the American representative. Prime Minister Lester Pearson chose Galbraith to be the Canadian one. "After I negotiated with myself on the few serious points of difference," Galbraith wrote, "I rendered a judgment satisfactory to the carriers of both countries."

137
Yousuf Karsh (1908-   )

In his memoirs, "Karsh of Ottawa" good-naturedly tells a couple of stories at his own expense. For example, his command of English was still imperfect when he photographed his first governor-general, Lord Bessborough, to whom he said, "Your Excellency, please recline in the reception room with my secretary." Another governor-general, Lord Tweedsmuir, listened with amusement when Karsh tactlessly suggested that the King (George VI) might wish to pose in another part of Rideau Hall where the light would be kinder to him.

But he seems to have received worse faux pas from his famous sitters than he committed.

"May I ask what nationality you are?" asked George Bernard Shaw.

Karsh, who came to Canada to escape oppression by the Turks, answered that he was Armenian by birth and proudly so.

"Good!" Shaw said. "I have many friends among the Armenians. But the only way to keep them healthy and strong is to have them exterminated every once in a while!"

138
Stanley Knowles (1908-   )

Knowles and Tommy Douglas often remarked on similarities in their backgrounds and careers. Both were early pioneers of the CCF and both reared in Winnipeg. Both sought political office in 1935. Both were rural by heritage and temperament; both believers in the so-called social gospel. Both were preachers and, prior to that, Linotype operators, and, prior to that, printers. The difference, Knowles liked to point out, was that whereas each kept up his legal status as a clergyman, only he himself continued to pay dues to the International Typographical Union. "Tommy's a Scot", he would explain.

139
Bud McDougald (1908-78)

John A. (Bud) McDougald was one of the founders of Argus Corporation and the second in the line of famous capitalists to run it (following E.P. Taylor and preceding Conrad Black). He practised a lifestyle commensurate with a communist's angriest vision of plutocracy. For example, he kept a stable of thirty-five rare automobiles. One of his first acquisitions was a Vauxhall sports car in which he once gave Mackenzie King a lift. The date was 1926. The teenager and the prime minister had met in downtown Toronto and the former offered to drive the latter up Yonge Street to a meeting with Ontario's chief justice, Sir William Mulock (who on his hundredth birthday would tell an interviewer, "I'm not in the habit of looking back—I leave that till I get old"). Along the way, the car's brakes seized. McDougald sought help but got only the use of a pair of bolt cutters, with which he then severed all the brake cables. The journey resumed with King petrified "even though I explained that I could brake quite easily, by changing down through the gears." But King remained "in a funk the whole time, clinging to the side of the car."

140
Hal Banks (1909-85)

The prominent hoodlum and trade union leader, remembered by history for his dictatorial stewardship of the Seafarers' International Union and the subsequent royal commission called to investigate it, was fond of a certain type of automobile. At one point in his Montreal years, before fleeing to the United States whence he had come, Banks admitted to having owned thirty-three Cadillacs at various times, including one whose bonnet he stoved in (for Banks was a heavy-set man) in a dive from a second-storey window during a fire. In the same period, he also had a power boat. When another vessel passed it in the water, Banks, who had every reason to be security conscious, bought a second one that was faster than the first. Both were paid for by union funds. When an underling pointed out the impropriety of this arrangement, Banks countered that he wasn't charging the union any dockage fees when they were moored at his lakeside hideaway.

141
John Glassco (1909-81)

When she was living in Paris in 1928, the American novelist Kay Boyle became acquainted with Buffy Glassco, the Canadian poet who would one day, in his *Memoirs of Montparnasse,* describe the *milieu* so memorably. For a time, the two writers had the same employer, the financially embarrassed Princess Dayang Muda of Sarawak, who hired them to help her with her autobiography. Boyle recalls that she was puzzled when Glassco, "on entering the salon", took to bowing "stiffly from the waist" before speaking to the princess and her consort and always "stood at a distance from them, near the grand piano, nervously refusing to sit down as he had done before." She added: "I concluded this must be a belated awareness of the deference a Canadian owes to British royalty, and I felt I must respect this and not discuss it with him. It was only long, long after that Buffy told me he had begun slipping gramophone records from the Princess' collection inside his jacket every day, and he had to move with caution to avoid breaking them. The records compensated for what he had not been paid, and the sale of them in the Quarter was usually enough to buy his supper that night."

142
Malcolm Lowry (1909-57)

It was in North Vancouver that the novelist completed his masterpiece, *Under the Volcano*. He arrived in 1940 and eventually took to living in a beach shack at Dollarton where he had a view of "the loveliest of oil refineries". He received a tiny regular income from England, just enough to let him qualify as a remittance man. Much of it seems to have gone towards alcohol, particularly Bols gin, which, as one literary pilgrim recalls, sometimes replaced tea and coffee in the Lowry household. A mixture of Bols and seawater, it is said, led another such visitor, the critic A.J.M. Smith, to jump from the window fully clothed into Burrard Inlet. Al Purdy tells of a visit he paid in 1954, Lowry's last year in Canada. They had helped to consume the only three bottles of liquor on hand and so proceeded to a liquor store at Main and Hastings where Lowry bought six units of his beloved Bols. He then instructed Purdy, who was driving, to head for a certain church whose stained-glass he, Lowry, had long admired. On arriving, they found a wedding in progress. The officiating clergyman seemed displeased to see the two literary men, and Purdy sought to placate him. With his friend thus occupied, Lowry slipped away and was later found kneeling in drunken prayer with the six gin-bottles in the pew behind him. Some months later, after Lowry's departure for England, Purdy and two others went to the shack once more and poured what remained of a bottle of wine off the end of Lowry's dock. It was a gesture of farewell and remembrance, and a prescient one. After he left Canada, Lowry accelerated his race towards self-destruction and died in 1957.

143
Roy Ward Dickson (1910-   )

Dickson was a former teacher who had devised a sort of game for his students, with skill-testing questions designed to reveal the breadth of their general knowledge. Later, he tried and failed to syndicate a column based on the same idea to newspapers across the country. Then one Depression evening, when he was working as an advertising salesman for the Toronto *Daily Star,* he hit upon the idea of adapting the notion for radio and adding prizes for the winners. "I pictured whole families gathered about their sets, competing among themselves, yelling out answers, actually *participating* in what was going on many miles away. Simultaneously learning, and having fun." He purchased time on a local radio station and persuaded three sponsors to buy commercials.

"On May 15th, 1935, 'Professor Dick and his Question Box' hit the airwaves.

"It was the world's first quiz show.

"Within two years, there were over two hundred of them being aired in North America alone, and a great many more elsewhere."

144
Hume Cronyn (1911-   )

Many theatrical figures have devised personal solutions to the recurring diplomatic problem of how to congratulate a colleague on a lacklustre performance without being a hypocrite. W.S. Gilbert, for example, would exclaim as follows: "My dear chap! Good isn't the word!" Cronyn's technique is more subtle. He enters the dressing room with a friendly smile and a steady gaze and then, grasping the actor by the shoulder, says, "How about you?"

145
Jack Kent Cooke (1912-   )

Cooke was an early business partner of the first Lord Thomson. He later acquired the country's biggest radio station and a number of magazines including *Saturday Night*. From those relatively small beginnings, he went on to become an important entrepreneur in American communications and sporting circles, owner of the Washington Redskins and the Los Angeles Lakers (and of the Lakers' home, the Forum). He also owns the Chrysler Building in New York.

Hugh Garner, the novelist, worked for Cooke's assorted Toronto enterprises and would credit Cooke with being his mentor in matters of fashion.

"He once collared me in his office—he and I were both high school dropouts and the same age—and showed me a book he was studying on 'taste', asking me which of four illustrations in the book was the most tasteful. I pointed one out, and he congratulated me and told me it was the same one he had chosen. On another occasion he asked me how to pronounce the word 'dour' and I pronounced it 'dower'. 'So did I, Hugh, until I just found out it's pronounced 'dooer'. He used to buy his clothes at Brooks Bros. in New York, we were both in our late thirties and early forties at the time, and I stuck to Daks English clothes. One day I went to the office wearing a loud large-checked sports jacket, a real coat-of-many-colors. Jack said 'Where in hell did you buy that goddam Macinaw, fer chrissakes!' He was wearing a Brooks Bros. American tweed sports jacket that looked like something he picked up in a department store bargain basement, though for once I kept my mouth shut."

146
Irving Layton (1912-   )

Aviva Layton has told of accompanying her future husband on a pilgrimage to Shakespeare and Company during a stay in Paris in 1959. The famous bookstore, where so many writers of the 1920s held court, had long since passed from Sylvia Beach's hands to those of George Whitman, another American expatriate. Whitman invited the Canadian couple for coffee in the building's loft, accessible by ladder from the art gallery located immediately above the ground-floor bookshop. Layton was suffering from gastric distress he attributed to rich French food and stepped out onto the corrugated tin roof to relieve himself. The roof gave way. With his trousers still at half mast, Layton went crashing into the gallery where, in his companion's recollection, "a *vernissage* or something was going on."

They later repaired the roof, carrying building materials across the city when no taxi would accept them, but the proprietor was not forgiving. "What an animal!" he kept repeating.

147
Rear Admiral Jeffrey Brock (1913-   )

Brock commanded Canada's destroyers in the Korean War and resigned from the Royal Canadian Navy in the 1960s to protest the Unification Act. He had earlier had a distinguished and varied naval career during the Second World War, in successive command of a number of British and Canadian vessels that took part in the North Atlantic convoys. He has repeated the story of the one corvette that signalled another during a gale WHAT DO YOU MAKE OF OUR POSITION?, to which came the reply DON'T KNOW. AM A STRANGER HERE MYSELF. It was during such escort duty, when tempers were as short as quarters were cramped, that he hit upon an innovative method of expressing displeasure with an officer's performance in such a way as not to ignite a volatile situation. In contravention of regulations he would wear a red waistcoat beneath his jacket. "Communicating severe displeasure with the actions of one of my officers became a simple matter of unbuttoning my uniform jacket and 'flashing scarlet'."

148
Hugh Garner (1913-79)

"I forget what year it was [wrote the author of the novel *Cabbagetown* and other such works of realism], but I attended the Danforth Avenue Businessmen's annual picnic in East Toronto's Withrow Park one evening just as a Master-of-Ceremonies was asking contestants for a quiz contest to step up on the stage. My only previous stage experience had been in my very early teens, when I won first prize in a Charleston dancing contest in a Parliament Street movie house, long torn down to make room to build the Regent Park Housing Project.

Anyhow, at the businessmen's picnic I and several older male contestants mounted the stage for the quiz show.

"One by one they were eliminated, unable to answer questions like: 'Name the German general who helped Wellington defeat Napoleon at Waterloo', 'What are both cross-threads of a piece of fabric called?', 'Who invented the cotton gin?' and other such esoteric trivia that was right up my alley. I answered them easily: General von Blucher, the warp and woof, Eli Whitney. Finally I was the last contestant on the stage, and I could see that the M.C. wasn't happy that the shabby kid standing alone in front of him had eliminated all the local Danforth Avenue dudes, some of whom may have been his friends. He searched through his question cards for the one final question I had to answer to win, hoping, I suppose, it would be the one that would eliminate me too. The prize was a Tip Top Tailors custom-made suit, and I not only needed a suit, custom-made or not, but I wasn't going to allow any Danforth businessman scissorbill to beat me out of the prize.

"He'd probably have beaten me on a question demanding job expertise or dealing in physics or chemistry, none of which were my strong points, but out of his own stupidity he picked not the toughest question but the one that needed the longest answer. I can see him leering down at me yet, probably either an undertaker or a florist, who seem to have been our perennial aldermen and controllers in the city government from what was then Toronto's Ward One.

"He gave the crowd a supercilious aldermanic grin, turned to me and spat out 'Name the forty-eight states of the United States!'

"I had him! American geography has always been my forte.

"I stepped up to the microphone and began: 'Maine, New Hampshire, Vermont, Massachusetts, Rhode Island, Connecticut, New York....' I almost missed Delaware, but put it in after Virginia rather than ahead of it. I could see him ticking them off on his answer card, as the crowd was as silent as the crowd that watched David slingshot Goliath.

"'…Montana, Wyoming, Colorado, New Mexico, Arizona, Utah, Idaho….'

"There were a few titters from the crowd, and the M.C.'s face began to purple with embarrassed apoplexy.

"I finished going south to north along the Pacific coast, 'California, Oregon and Washington.'

"The Master-of-Ceremonies cried triumphantly, 'You missed Maryland!'

"I said into the microphone, 'I did like hell!'

"Some of the crowd laughed, and others began to boo. One big guy from down on Empire Avenue stepped to the platform steps. I knew him as a man who worked at the Eastern Avenue gasworks and also played amateur softball in a small field at the foot of Logan Avenue. He shouted up to the purple face of the M.C., who stepped back a couple of paces, 'I know the kid said Maryland, because I play the horses at Laurel, and I was waiting for him to name the state. He's won fair and square.'

"The crowd began shouting, 'Sure he did! Give him the prize, you phony bastard!' and a few other south-end-of-the-ward compliments.

"The Master-of-Ceremonies, seeing not only his Rotary honesty but a hundred future votes slipping away from him, handed me a voucher for a suit from Tip Top Tailors, and I read it, stuffed it into my pocket, and jumped down into the crowd where several members of the Riverdale Park gang were waiting. Later in the evening somebody unknown to me let the air out of the tires of the M.C.'s car that was parked on Carlaw Avenue. I have no doubt it was somebody from my south-end neighborhood. I don't think any of my neighbors ever liked any of our aldermen, especially those who were undertakers or florists."

149
George Ignatieff (1913-   )

Lester Pearson recruited George Ignatieff into the foreign service during the Second World War and they became fast friends. The relationship grew especially strong one Sunday morning during the Blitz "when we peered through the smoke-filled air at the devastation all around Canada House and agreed to dedicate our lives to a search for peace." Years later, when Pearson was a power in federal politics, he confided to Ignatieff that he had had a disturbing dream. "He dreamt, he told me, that he was attending his own funeral. What bothered him was not the thought of dying, but the sight of a gun carriage, muffled drums, and flags at half-mast—all the pomp usually associated with state funerals."

Pearson was puzzled as to the dream's significance.

"Mike, you've had a premonition," Ignatieff told him. "Some day you will be prime minister, and when you die, the country will give you a state funeral."

150
Stuart Keate (1913-   )

The journalist and newspaper executive, who in time became the publisher of the Vancouver *Sun,* demonstrated his interest in news at a tender age. "On the evening of September 14, 1923, I was listening to a radio broadcast of the heavyweight boxing championship between Jack Dempsey and Luis Firpo, 'The Wild Bull of the Pampas'. When Firpo knocked Dempsey out of the ring I dashed into nearby Granville Street and stopped the first car I could find. 'What's up, son?' asked the driver. 'Firpo has just knocked out Dempsey and won the heavyweight championship of the world,' I cried. Which, in retrospect, was an authentic harbinger of the career to come: I was not only first with the news, but had it totally wrong."

151
Edwin Alonzo Boyd (1914-   )

Boyd, the son of a police constable, became the country's most infamous bankrobber. He was leader of the Boyd Gang which terrorized (and titillated) southern Ontario in the late 1940s and early 1950s. The gang was the object of the largest manhunt in Canadian history following its escape from a Toronto jail in 1952, and most of the reverse adoration was focused on Boyd, who was handsome and athletic as well as resourceful. He was, however, no overnight success, having begun criminal life in the 1930s with a series of petty break-and-enter convictions.

During his first penitentiary term, in Prince Albert, Saskatchewan, Boyd learned to manipulate the bureaucracy. It was the custom to send inmates to work on the prison farm even in the winter. Boyd sent the warden an anonymous letter warning him that Boyd had been overheard plotting a breakout. He thus assured himself of lighter and warmer work indoors. His decision to specialize in robbing banks was quite deliberate, he would admit later. In 1948, he chanced upon a story in one of the Toronto newspapers about a mentally handicapped sixteen-year-old boy who had stuck up a bank and made off with $69,000. The youth had been apprehended only because he had not bothered to flee the scene but merely walked away at a normal pace. Noting the size of the jackpot, and taking into account what he considered his own superior talents, Boyd knew that he would do well in this fast-growing field.

152
Robert Stanfield (1914-   )

Stanfield became leader of the Nova Scotia Conservatives in 1946 when the party held no seats in the legislature. He gradually improved its performance until finally he formed the government ten years later (remaining premier until he entered federal politics in 1967). It was at the time of one such early campaign that George Nowlan, the Tories' national party president, suggested that Stanfield might benefit from the advice of Dalton Camp, who had been struggling successfully against Liberal supremacy in New Brunswick. Camp found Stanfield's Halifax law office thinly appointed, not to say gloomy, and the man himself infuriatingly low-keyed. Camp asked about the prospects of the election and Stanfield replied that, though his people were not actually running with the avowed purpose of getting trounced, losing was nonetheless their expectation. He went on to imply that a decrease in the humiliation of the defeat with each successive election was tantamount to victory of a kind. Such an attitude could only prove puzzling and offensive to Camp, with his combination of aggressive optimism and backroom cunning. Camp reported to Nowlan that though Stanfield did indeed need help, he should probably seek it elsewhere as the two Maritimers were sure to grate on each other's nerves.

"That's just what he needs, old boy", Nowlan replied. And so it proved to be.

153
Charles Templeton (1915-   )

The future broadcaster and writer of popular fiction was a lowly nineteen-year-old newspaper cartoonist with a grade nine education when he became a born-again Christian. He took to preaching and in a few years he became one of the most popular travelling evangelists in North America and a favourite religious personality of the mainstream media. He held the position, as he would admit later, despite increasing doubts about his faith, some of them brought on by reading such writers as Bertrand Russell. On one occasion he and his friend and colleague Billy Graham were scheduled to conduct a special service for American armed forces personnel at Gander, Newfoundland. A misunderstanding about the nature of their calling resulted in repeated booing and cries of "Bring on the girls". There was no such satisfactory explanation, however, when, to what he later confessed was his astonishment, he actually succeeded in healing a crippled child and a woman fatally ill with cancer: cases which seemed to defy strict physiological and psychological explanation. But his private doubts persisted and he sought to deepen his religious education, spending three years at the Princeton Theological Seminary (after failing to convince Graham to join him there). He finally quit the ministry in 1957, proclaiming himself an agnostic.

154
Constance Tomkinson (1915-   )

Tomkinson, a Nova Scotian and the daughter of a United Church minister, achieved success in the 1930s as a dancer with the Folies Bergere in Paris. *Les girls,* as members of the company were called, were a polyglot group, many of whom mistakenly assumed that Tomkinson, being a Canadian, must be fluent in French as well as English and no doubt other languages as well. "'Ah,' they would say, *'la Canadienne!'* and drag me into some garbled discussion. I consistently let them down with wild and free translations, but they never lost their faith in my linguistic abilities. Confidences and grievances were poured in my ear. I became a sort of Mother Confessor. Their secrets were safe with me; they went in one ear and left the other, untranslated."

155
Jean Drapeau (1916-   )

The seven-term mayor of Montreal used to tell of passing through an airline terminal and seeing a vaguely familiar elderly man looking dispirited and lost. It took him a moment to recognize the passenger as Louis St. Laurent. "He wasn't out of office very long before he was forgotten". Drapeau would say sadly. To avoid the same fate, he went to extraordinarily complex lengths, often Machiavellian, sometimes comic, to hold onto power. "I was privileged to hear privately Mayor Drapeau's confidential relevations on how to gain and keep power in politics through the manipulation of friend and foe alike", Edward Heath, the former British prime minister, has said. "It was one of the most hilarious and exhilarating talks I have ever had with a politician." He added: "Unfortunately I proved to be singularly bad at following his example."

Drapeau wrote two "political wills" during his career. The first was during the October Crisis when he left written instructions that no ransom was to be paid if he were kidnapped by terrorists. The second was after the Montreal Olympics, his triumph and folly. It stipulated that the Olympic Stadium not be renamed in his memory immediately following his death. But if, twenty years after his passing, the tribute should still seem appropriate, then he or his ghost would accede to the wishes of the living and accept the draft.

156
Sydney Newman (1917-   )

Newman, the winner of many awards from a number of countries, was at various times a senior executive and producer with the CBC and the commissioner of the National Film Board. "On his office wall was a Jackson Pollock-like abstract, which I liked very much", remembers one writer who worked with him at the CBC. "Newman told me he had seen it in the artist's home but could not accept it as it was because it was too big for the wall space he had in mind. He then asked the artist to cut off part of it, say three feet by five, which could fit between the wall and the door. The artist obliged at once." The story affected the writer's "confidence in the artistic visual standards waved about by him and his producers."

157
Norman Depoe (1918-80)

Depoe "was a top CBC newsman and pundit in his time and exuded a certain arrogance to go with undeniable competence", according to the journalist Peter Worthington, who observed him at close range during the Biafran civil war. He "had a bigger reputation in Canada than elsewhere, but saw no reason to change his style to blend with surroundings. However, what was acceptable or tolerated in Canada was not always appreciated in other countries, where neither his colleagues nor his interviewees were aware of his star status.

"Apparently Depoe went to Port Harcourt and got into a shouting match with Colonel Adekunle [of the Nigerian military] over whether or not he should be allowed to travel. The Black Scorpion [as Adekunle was known] did a bit of stinging of his own by forcing Depoe to stand on the tarmac of the airport for most of one day, unprotected from the scorching sun, without water or refreshment. Then he packed him on the evening flight back to Lagos. By that time Norman was dehydrated, deflated, and disconcerted. As one who liked Norman and who had been exposed to his sometimes haughty manner, I was more intrigued by than indignant at the episode, and felt that anyone who could do this to him couldn't be all bad."

158
Louis Dudek (1918-   )

The story of the first occasion on which the BBC telecast the most infamous of four-letter words is well known in Britain. The speaker was the drama critic Kenneth Tynan, a lifelong stutterer; it is alleged that what he actually said was "Fffff". The breakthrough for CBC Radio was a 1968 poetry reading being aired live by Robert Weaver, the corporation's head of literary programming. According to one of the participants, Robin Skelton, the atmosphere was charged with mischief and primed for profanity when "the doors at the back of the auditorium flew open and Milton Acorn made his entrance, unruffled, and smiling at the cries of 'Milt', 'Here's Milt!', 'He's here!' Frank Scott gave a crocodile-like grin, and as Milton reached his chair the show went on." Yet it was not Acorn, the professional rabblerouser, who disrupted the gentility of the event, but rather the considerably drier and more staid figure of Dudek, a professor at McGill University. "Cool, sardonic, poised and bland, he read a poem of such vitriolic humour and outrageous vocabulary that we gasped and hugged each other. The poem became more and more outrageous as it proceeded. We heard the word 'fuck' broadcast over the CBC airwaves for the first time. We heard the word 'shit'. We looked up and saw Bob Weaver in his glass-fronted control booth puffing on his pipe like a man demented and bouncing up and down with emotion. We weren't too sure why he was capering, but capering he certainly was. It was Dudek's evening. Purged, we applauded. Hopefully we searched the next day's papers for words of condemnation. There were none. The CBC had no complaints. We were staggered, and perhaps just a little mortified."

159
George Grant (1918-88)

One day in the 1970s, the conservative philosopher was deep in conversation with Dennis Lee the poet, Scott Symons the novelist and Charles Taylor the journalist, fellow nationalists who might be called his disciples.

"I started to read Céline when I was feeling down", Grant was saying. "I felt I was on the edge of a nervous breakdown..."

His wife interrupted. "Oh, George is always on the brink of one nervous breakdown or another. Usually he goes and reads the biography of some Anglican bishop."

160
Johnny Wayne (1918-) & Frank Shuster (1916-)

Paul Martin, the Liberal politician, recalls meeting the team of comedians in the lobby of the Park Plaza Hotel in Toronto sometime in the 1960s. He asked them if they had ever met Lester Pearson, with whom he had just concluded a meeting in a suite upstairs. "When they told me they had not, I decided to take them up and introduce them. We rehearsed a little skit: they were to pretend to be recently arrived immigrants to Canada, who had asked to see if Pearson could help bring their families into the country. Mike, working at a table in his dressing gown, did not recognize the two comics and was a little annoyed at being disturbed."

161
Igor Gouzenko (1919-82)

Gouzenko, in 1945 a lowly cipher clerk in the Soviet embassy in Ottawa, became famous to a generation when he defected and revealed the existence of elaborate Russian spy-networks in North America. In exchange for his testimony, he received a new name and identity. He did not melt into history, however, but for the next forty years was conspicuous, at intervals, as a litigious sort of public personality, hiding his face beneath a white hood because he feared assassination. Few Canadians who saw him without this trademark mask knew they were seeing Igor Gouzenko. Conversely, few who watched the shrouded figure on television or at public events would ever glimpse the features of the person underneath. At one period about 1950, however, Gouzenko sometimes called on an editor at *Saturday Night,* and Hugh Garner, who worked there at the time, remembered having the visitor pointed out to him. "A couple of months later I was walking through Simpson's department store when I saw Gouzenko standing at a counter. He was no longer accompanied by his RCMP bodyguards as he had been at the beginning, and I walked up behind him and in a conversational tone said, 'Hello, Igor'. I was afraid he was going to jump out of his shoes."

162
Pierre Elliott Trudeau (1919-)

Trudeau and the members of his first cabinet were sworn in on April 19, 1968, and a cabinet meeting was held later that same day. One of the new ministers recalls wondering "how my old friend was going to look as he took his place in the Voltaire armchair" reserved for him at the long table. The PM began in business-like, even clinical, fashion. "Gentleman," he said, "I'm not going to linger over preliminaries. We have quite a lot of work before us. We might as well get at it without..." He interrupted himself and examined the two-piece headrest on his chair. "Strange, these things make a kind of echo! I'll have to get used to it", he said.

163
Dalton Camp (1920-   )

Camp will forever be best known for his part, when he was the national president of the Progressive Conservative Party, in ousting John Diefenbaker as leader. But the way in which he disproved a biblical injunction, by refusing to perish by the sword (several wounds notwithstanding), must also be recalled in order to be marvelled at. In the 1970s he surfaced as the supreme political journalist, one whose wit revealed truth rather than hid it, and whose candour, being all-pervasive, was difficult to distinguish from the opposite in other people.

"Over the years of Diefenbaker's ascendancy and decline," he wrote with characteristic frankness but with a sort of self-deprecation-at-others'-expense, "my Toronto office—otherwise and ostensibly an advertising agency—became a clearing house, talent bank, hiring hall and recruiting office for the Tory party; even a confessional (not merely in jest had [Manitoba Premier, now Senator] Duff Roblin once called me 'the lay pope of conservatism')."

It might be said fairly that as a commentator Camp has never been easier on his friends than on himself. Fainter praise than that he gave Paul Hellyer, for example, would have to be written in invisible ink. Hellyer and he, Camp stated, "are both lapsed Grits, sometime columnists and—a harder truth—failed politicians. The Don Quixote of Canadian politics, Hellyer has enriched its history with the humours of his romantic, earnest visions. But when he is not running for office, or holding one, Hellyer is easy to like." Camp went on to record that when, as part of the entertainment at a political dinner in 1979, Hellyer broke out into song, he was "awarded an ovation larger than any given him at either Grit or Tory leadership conventions" where he had been seeking the leadership. Apparent friendship restrained him from mentioning the party Hellyer had gone on to found in frustration after trying the other two.

164
William Hutt (1920-   )

In 1973, the Stratford Festival production of *King Lear* was performed in the Soviet Union with the original Canadian cast, including Hutt in the title role. A Toronto theatre critic accompanied them. Hutt complained to the manager of their Moscow hotel after learning that the writer had been put up in a suite while he, the star, made do with a mere room. The manager explained, through an interpreter, that the reviewer was an on-looker and therefore a guest. By contrast, Hutt, being an actor, was a worker, and so was being honoured with a worker's accommodation.

165
Edmund Carpenter (1922-   )

The Canadian anthropologist (with whom Marshall McLuhan was associated in the magazine *Explorations*) makes the point in his pioneer work in the Arctic that the Inuit, with their strong oral tradition, are able to retain a foreign language such as English even though they might not use it for long periods. He tells of a hunter named Ohnainewk who had been taught a little English by a Mountie's wife in 1910. Although he had little opportunity to practise it in the intervening years, he was firmly in command of its subtleties when Carpenter spent time with him at Southhampton Island, Northwest Territories, in 1952.

"The wind is cold", Carpenter said in the native dialect.

Ohnainewk laughed and answered in English.

"How can the *wind* be cold? You're cold; you're unhappy. But the wind isn't cold or unhappy."

166
René Lévesque (1922-87)

The animosity that linked René Lévesque and Pierre Trudeau not only predated their respective roles as premier of Quebec and prime minister of Canada but actually appears to have transcended mere questions of federalism, biculturalism and Quebec independence. One might venture to say that for decades before their public confrontations came to a head, each played Sherlock Holmes to the other's Dr Moriarty in a complicated interior melodrama.

Their first meeting was in 1954 or 1955 when Trudeau, a left-wing lawyer in private practice, was editing *Cité libre,* the political review he had founded, and Lévesque was at the height of his renown as a television journalist of the loftier sort (so that in his first election campaign he would have difficulty shaking the popular image that he was an artist). His fellow journalist Gérard Pelletier brought him to the Radio-Canada canteen in Montreal to meet Trudeau. Lévesque offered to contribute to the new journal. "Very good," Trudeau replied, "but allow me one simple question: Can you write?"

The remark was a prophylaxis. It prevented any friendship from developing between them despite the interests, opinions and views they shared at the time.

Following the death of their nemesis, Premier Maurice Duplessis, in 1959, Lévesque, Trudeau, Pelletier and the labour leader Jean Marchand all were approached to enter provincial politics and help move Quebec beyond the Deplessis heritage of corruption and repression. All considered the offer, but Trudeau, Pelletier and Marchand declined in turn, opting instead for federal politics, where they would comprise, in Lévesque's view, a kind of unholy trinity. Lévesque of course accepted.

167
Jack McClelland (1922-   )

In his long career with McClelland & Stewart, a firm founded by his father, the Toronto book publisher Jack McClelland cultivated a flamboyant personal image and a flair for clever promotions. In 1980, for example, he announced plans for a Roman-style party to celebrate the appearance of *The Emperor's Virgin,* a historical novel by Sylvia Fraser. Clad in togas, the publisher and the author descended Yonge Street in a chariot, moving towards the bookstore where the function was to be held. A freak snowstorm impeded their progress, however, and when they arrived a coy breeze played with their flimsy white costumes. "Jack must be slowing down", one local wag was moved to observe. "Only one sheet to the wind."

168
Jeanne Sauvé (1922-   )

Jeanne Sauvé did not expect to be offered a portfolio by Pierre Trudeau following the 1972 general election. Women were still a novelty in federal politics if no longer a rarity (as late as 1980 there were only fourteen female MPs). In any event, only two women had ever sat in Cabinet: Ellen Fairclough, named by Diefenbaker in 1957, and Judy LaMarsh, chosen by Pearson in 1963. In all the vast pool of obviously qualified Liberal MPs, then, she was almost certainly the only one not hoping, praying, for the ceremonial telephone call from the prime minister. On the day in question she in fact had her phone off the hook while she caught up on her correspondence. The prime minister's office had to ring her husband at work. He dashed home by taxi to tell his spouse to put the receiver back in its cradle. She became minister of Science and Technology.

By 1979, she had grown cannier. Trudeau telephoned and said, "Jeanne, as a minister you're going to be forgotten once you leave politics, but you'll never be forgotten as the first woman Speaker."

"If I say no", she asked, "will I be in the Cabinet?"

Trudeau assured her that she would.

"What portfolio?"

"That I'm not telling you", he replied.

Among her first acts after becoming Speaker of the House of Commons was to have her Montreal *couturier* design her a new uniform. She feared that the traditional one, with its black robe, black tricorn and white gloves, might make her look like a transvestite.

At the end of 1983, Trudeau asked her if she would become Canada's first female governor general. "It was such a great honour, there was no way I could refuse", she recalled. "I didn't even say, like you would about a cabinet post, 'I'll think about it' or 'I'll see if I can handle it.' I accepted immediately." Trudeau suggested she might wish to discuss the offer with her husband. "No, I don't think I should delay my answer", she replied. "It's such an honour I will say yes right away."

169
Fr Leonard Boyle (1923-   )

In 1984, Fr Boyle of the Pontificial Institute for Medieval Studies in Toronto became the first Canadian, indeed the first non-European, to head the Biblioteca Apostolica Vaticana—the Vatican Library. The announcement spurred recollection of an occasion in the late 1960s when he was about to enter the library in the company of a student, a young woman he had met along the way. He had been doing research in the institution for years, but this time found his progress barred because of the way his companion was dressed. Miniskirts, explained the Swiss Guard, were not permitted inside. Whereupon Fr Boyle, using extreme eloquence and convoluted logic, convinced him to bend the rules by averaging the length of the mini in question and his own ankle-length Dominican habit. Both visitors were admitted.

170
Kenneth Thomson, 2nd Baron Thomson of Fleet (1923-   )

The heir to the Thomson title and the Thomson newspaper empire was touring Australia and New Zealand in 1955 with a group of Commonwealth media executives but left earlier than planned, he confided to a colleague, because he missed his fiancée, to whom he had written twenty-eight letters during the past twenty-three days without yet receiving any from her. The friend later asked the future Lady Thomson if she had read all twenty-eight. "Most of them", was her reply.

171
Lloyd Bochner (1924-   )

Although not yet a film actor, Bochner was already well known during the Second World War because of *Fighting Navy,* a CBC Radio drama in which he starred while actually serving in the Royal Canadian Navy.

One of his fellow sailors remembers: "Bochner spotted me one evening trying to iron my navy uniform. In the navy the creases are on the sides and turn inward. I'd never ironed anything before, even with creases on the outside, and was laboriously trying to re-iron creases to turn inward. Bochner, with the patience of an old hand of two months, showed me how to iron the uniform inside out, thus creating creases that turn inward. I thought it the most brilliant bit of information I'd ever heard – and certainly the most useful at that moment. Bochner more or less had the run of *HMCS York,* with even officers and petty officers occasionally seeking his autograph."

172
Max Ferguson (1924-   )

The broadcaster recalls the day when, in December 1946, as the newest member of the staff at the CBC in Halifax, he created his most memorable character:

"With a desperation born of despair and with just twenty seconds to air time, I hit on the idea of disguising my voice by dropping the register, thrusting out my jaw, and clamping my back teeth together. As I pushed down the microphone switch, out came the words, 'Howdy! Welcome to *After Breakfast Breakdown,*' in a low, aged, hard, flat, sloppily sibilant voice that surprised even myself. 'This is your old pal Rawhide,' I continued, pulling the name out of the air on the spur of the moment, although I'd heard it used once or twice in my life to denote a type of tough, untanned leather."

The spirit of invention had taken hold, and for the next half hour Ferguson made spurious introductions to the various country songs he was being paid to announce. He overstepped the bounds, however, in calling the Yodelling Ranger, the most popular country performer in the Maritimes, the Yodelling Idiot, and was forced to apologize.

"I just made a very unfortunate mistake in calling the previous singer the Yodelling Idiot", he told the listeners. "I certainly didn't mean to be disparaging and was obviously confusing him with *another* Yodelling Idiot I once knew in Upper Canada.

"This is the Canadian Broadcasting Corporation."

173
Judy LaMarsh (1924-80)

"I am publicity-prone, just as some people are accident-prone", claimed the Liberal MP for Niagara Falls. She was also a strong force for women in Canadian public life, though never a mere "sop to women voters". Hers was a fierce but quiet battle, often conducted behind closed doors and clenched teeth.

By the end of three years in politics she had acquired not only high visibility but a reputation for wading into difficult jobs, and had been led to expect a Cabinet position after the Pearson Liberals bounded to power in 1963. She had always sworn to herself, however, not to accept any portfolio once held by Ellen Fairclough, lest people "draw unhappy comparisons" (though, as she admitted later, no one ever seemed tempted to do so—perhaps no one dared). Nonetheless she was disappointed when offered Health and Welfare, even though it gave her the opportunity to make a lasting contribution in the form of the Canada Pension Plan.

After the 1965 general election, Pearson offered her a choice of three posts — postmaster general or secretary of state (both the former property of Fairclough) or solicitor general. LaMarsh went against her own longstanding pledge and became the secretary of state. She occupied the job during Centennial year and was thus obliged to compromise another of her beliefs.

Not only did women members of Parliament not enjoy privileges equal to those of male MPs, who received free haircuts and the like; they were expected to curtsy rather than bow on certain ceremonial occasions, such as when acknowledging the governor general or certain foreign heads of state. This had always rankled LaMarsh, who was later attacked for bowing to His Excellency Roland Michener. Her objection on principle was, she confessed, strengthened by the fact that she "could rarely, in performing a curtsy, manage to land on the right foot." Now with potentates and princes flooding the country for the Centennial, she "had to execute more of them during the year than any other woman." She kept her chagrin to herself, however, and made a complete success of July 1, 1967.

The gown she wore to the state dinner was presented subsequently to the National Museum. With the level of directness and candour that made her so memorable, LaMarsh recalled that she "was tempted to have its pale green, corded silk folds reduced by a third so that history will not record this woman politician as being quite so king-sized."

174
William Stevenson (1924-   )

The success of *A Man Called Intrepid* and Stevenson's other books has tended to obscure, rather than highlight, that which so frequently informs them: the author's previous life as a foreign correspondent. Between 1949 and 1956 he was conspicuous in the world's trouble spots on behalf of the Toronto *Star* and would later do the same work for *The Globe and Mail*. At the former paper expecially, he enjoyed an additional and purely intramural renown for his imaginative way with expense-account vouchers. "My method", he has said, "was simply to add up at the end how much of the paper's money I'd spent and then make up something plausible—or not so plausible. Once, coming home from India for the *Star,* I found I was still $50 short on the tally." This was long before the word *guru* had entered the English language. "So I listed two gurus for that amount. I attached a note saying that gurus were normally $50 apiece but that, being conscious of the *Star*'s economy drive just then, I'd made a special bargain." The item was approved. Another famous Stevenson expense account included the following entry: "Helicopter crash, $22." This time there was no elaboration. Again, the claim was passed.

175
Ross McLean (1925-87)

McLean was the *enfant terrible* of Canadian television, renowned equally for his discovery of young talent, his innovative programming and his running war with the CBC (which he called "the bind that ties"). He was one of the people who helped create television in English Canada in 1952, and though he quit the corporation several times he was suspended only once. The incident followed an instalment of *Tabloid,* one of the groundbreaking public affairs shows with which he was associated (others were *Close-Up, The Way It Is* and *Quest*). A Montreal viewer had written to complain about the previous week's broadcast and McLean superimposed the correspondent's address on the screen, with the tacit suggestion that the audience rebuke the man for his criticism. The writer of the letter, a physician, was inundated for days with crank calls and hate messages, taxis he did not summon and pizzas he had not ordered. McLean was suspended until he apologized, which took three weeks. "The CBC has many enemies", he said. "Among them, itself."

176
John Neville (1925-)

Don Rubin, the theatre critic, was interviewing Neville on the CBC. Unable to restrain his curiosity any longer, he concluded the session by asking why Neville was wearing an earring.

"Because I thought two earrings might look effeminate", Neville replied.

177
Betty Kennedy (1926-)

In 1959, the year she began her broadcasting career, Kennedy was living frugally in Ottawa with her husband and four children, picking up small television appearances and helping to organize fashion shows while she waited for better opportunities to materialize. Crawley Films was producing a television series about the Mounties, shot in the Gatineau Hills, and Kennedy was convinced that she had been discovered at last when she received a telephone call from the producer asking if she could come to work. In a calculated after-thought, the producer asked that she bring along Chief, the family's golden retriever. As it happened, the dog previously used in the series had taken to biting its human co-star. So it was Chief that was being groomed for the big time, not Kennedy. Instead she arrived each morning at seven and spent the day loitering in the cold while Chief did his stuff between stays in a warm dressing room with a star on the door. The production company took out an insurance policy for Chief through Lloyd's. Its coverage, said Kennedy, exceeded that enjoyed by all the other members of the family combined. But come payday, Kennedy said, "I got the cheque, though."

178
Margaret Laurence (1926-87)

When she was a student at United College in Winnipeg, she couldn't afford to purchase Canadian books but "read Gabrielle Roy, Hugh MacLennan, Morley Callaghan, and others, in the book department of the Hudson's Bay Company, just across the road from the college, a chapter at a time, hoping the sales clerk wouldn't notice us standing there, turning pages. A rather touching footnote to this story is that when I first met Dale Zieroth, the talented poet who was born in the same town as I was, just 20 years after myself, and who grew up on a farm, near Glenella, Manitoba, he told me that when *he* was at United College, he couldn't afford to buy books, either, so he read my novel, *A Jest of God,* in the bookstore at the Bay, a chapter at a time, hoping the sales clerk wouldn't notice."

179

A visitor was browsing in the library at Laurence's home and came upon the copy of *Paradise Lost* she had used as a student, complete with her marginal notes. Next to the passage

For contemplation he and valour formed;
For softness she and sweet attractive grace,
He for God only, she for God in him:
His fair large front and eye sublime declared
Absolute rule

she had scribbled, "All too typical".

The guest flipped forward a few pages.

The poet had written:

Hail wedded love, mysterious law, true source
Of human offspring, sole propriety,
In Paradise of all things common else.

Beside this was another comment in Laurence's hand: "Ha! I wonder what Mrs. Milton would say."

180

Jim Pattison (1928-)

The Vancouver business tycoon got a job as a used car salesman when he was nineteen and enrolled at the University of British Columbia. It was his practice to drive an automobile to school each morning, sell it to a fellow student during the day and return home by public transportation in the evening. Later, in 1955, when he took over management of his father's used-car business, he initiated the practice (subsequently notorious) of firing the salesman who sold the fewest cars each month. "The best salesman hasn't been hired yet", he would say.

181

Jerry Goodis (1929-)

Goodis, a prolific founder of advertising agencies, is also perforce an optimist. "If anyone asks Jerry the time," one of his partners has said, "he thinks he's getting the Bulova account."

182
Peter C. Newman (1929-)

When Newman was following John Diefenbaker's progress on the hustings in preparation for writing *Renegade in Power,* he met a young reporter named John Fraser during a stop in Newfoundland. "After we had talked for a few minutes", recalled Fraser, who eventually became the editor of *Saturday Night,* "he told me I could tag along and I spent the next six hours watching this consummate observer dart in and around the Diefenbaker campaign. I watched as he drew out people in conversation and flattered them with his interest, how he handled the difficult and precarious business of taking notes, how he never professed to know very much of anything so that his informants never took anything for granted. In this way he gleaned all sorts of useful trivia and footnote material, which is such a feature of his books."

183
Mario Amaya (1933-86)

For a period in the late 1960s and early 1970s, Amaya, a stylish and innovative figure on the Anglo-American art scene, was the curator of the Art Gallery of Ontario (where a portrait of him by David Hockney hangs). He sometimes outraged and frequently puzzled the benefactors of that institution, which only a generation earlier had been thought of as a sort of private culture preserve for the local establishment. One of his small but characteristic gestures was exhibiting a live cow and a painting of a cow side by side. In 1968, just before accepting the position, he had been fortunate enough to be at Andy Warhol's studio in New York on the day a self-described feminist terrorist burst in with a handgun, wounding both the artist and his visitor. The incident permitted Amayato to telephone a hostess who was expecting him at a dinner party. "I'll be a little late", he reported with wonderful insouciance. "I've been shot."

184
Scott Symons (1933-   )

In 1962 this scion of a prominent Rosedale family and future scapegrace novelist attended a banquet at Rideau Hall in honour of the Queen Mother's visit to Ottawa. In the post-dinner chit-chat, the Queen Mother asked him when his people had come to Canada. "Two centuries ago, Ma'am, from the Thirteen Colonies, as Loyalists to your Crown", he told her. "We are still loyal to your Crown, Ma'am. We are Your Majesty's Royal Americans." Both parties wept.

185
David Suzuki (1936-   )

The famous scientist was invited to lunch at the Parliamentary Restaurant and arrived "in his accustomed attire: neat jeans, open-necked shirt and jacket." The maitre d' denied him entry.

"But I was allowed in here last week when I had lunch with the Minister of Communications", Suzuki protested.

The maitre d' explained to Suzuki's friend, "Ah yes, but that was when there were a whole bunch of his people here and we lifted the rules." Apparently Suzuki had been mistaken for a native Indian.

Suzuki and his companion ate at the Chateau Laurier instead.

186
Barbara Frum (1937-   )

In the 1970s, Frum was the host of *As It Happens,* a phone-out programme on CBC Radio, on which she routinely interviewed newsworthy persons while the news was underway. Examples might include the occasion she tracked down a politically motivated bank robber who was holding hostages in a New York financial institution, or the time she persuaded someone at New Scotland Yard to enter the women's loo and retrieve an eyewitness to an attack on Princess Anne.

A near-perfect example of her tenacious style came when she telephoned the British embassy in Reykjavik when the building was under seige from Icelandic cod fishermen.

"I'd like to speak to the British ambassador", she said.

"I am the ambassador", a voice replied, amid the sound of breaking glass.

"We understand there's a riot going on. What is that terrible noise in the background?"

"My windows, Madame."

"Ambassador, we'd like your view of the current dispute between your country and Iceland."

"My dear Madame, will you please get off my line. I have to telephone my Foreign Office."

"Please, just one moment. I need only one comment..."

"Madame, Madame, you don't seem to understand. I haven't yet reported to my own government. There's only one line out of here, which you are rudely monopolizing."

"Well, if you'll just answer my one question, I'll be glad to leave you to your duties."

Having no choice, the ambassador consented to be interviewed.

187
Tommy Hunter (1937-   )

Hunter began his professional life as a country singer on radio in 1953 and later the same year was part of a group called the Golden Prairie Cowboys. He was sixteen. To achieve a suitably mature look he was forced to shave part of his head to suggest a receding hairline. The Cowboys earned their living on Yonge Street in Toronto, performing in various places of low resort. Through some caprice they were once booked into a jazz club there. "Must have been quite a shock", Hunter has recalled, "for the regular audience to settle down for an evening of Miles Davis and get Bob Nolan and the Sons of the Pioneers instead!" What's more, they were expected to entertain on New Year's Eve. They soon found the jazz enthusiasts avoiding their particular tavern. But country fans, who previously had been widely scattered, started to concentrate around them. Hunter's perennial success was underway.

188
Joe Clark (1939-   )

"Poor Joe", observed a Liberal from the Opposition benches of the House of Commons in 1979. "Never does he appear comfortable as prime minister. And his ease in the House is not increased by one of our more portly members from Quebec who, with a great fog-horn voice but limited command of English, booms out whenever Joe attempts to speak, 'Sit down, Joe! You bad boy, Joe! You sit down, Joe!' And sometimes Joe does."

189
Brian Mulroney (1939-   )

In 1961, when he was a twenty-one-year-old university student, Mulroney was chosen as one of Canada's most promising young people for the purposes of a special issue of *Maclean's* devoted to that subject. He was interviewed by Peter Gzowski, who was himself not much older, and Peter C. Newman.

Newman quizzed him about the views of the sort of young person who would become the political leaders of the future. "What do you think will be his attitude towards patronage, for instance?"

"I think his attitude is going to be drastically changed from the attitude of those who are in government today", Mulroney answered. "The young people of today are going to strengthen the nation at the cost of partisan politics, and they are going to take a much more idealistic view of things twenty years from now than we do today."

190
Nancy Greene (1943-   )

The relentlessly perky alpine skier, two-time winner of the World Cup, was not free of professional aggravations as she climbed to the top of her sport in the 1960s. She has recounted how a sporting goods manufacturer arranged for members of the Canadian Olympic team to borrow skis when competing in the US. The athletes weren't aware they were supposed to declare the skis on their return to Canada. But Rod Hebron let slip the fact that the skis were simply on loan, and RCMP officers and Customs agents confiscated those of the entire contingent. "We'd violated some regulation or other and we had to pay duty as if the skis were purchases. And what was worse, we had to pay fines to get our skis back. I borrowed $400 from the bank to make my share, and then I took a job typing all summer to replay the bank."

Later, in July 1966, Greene took a nasty spill during the world championships in Portillo, Chile. "I was told later that I flipped through three cartwheels—at a speed of 40 m.p.h. My helmet flew off, my skis and poles shattered against the hard snow, and I crashed into the retaining wall around the course. For a few seconds I saw stars and I had to fight not to pass out. Officials and spectators swarmed around me and everyone had a piece of medical advice for me. I concentrated on staying conscious and on checking for broken limbs. I seemed to be able to move my arms and legs, even if they did register a terrible numbness, and, slowly, gingerly, I stood up. I managed to climb off the course, over the retaining wall, and then I looked up. The finish line was barely fifty yards away—fifty more yards, such a short distance, and I would almost certainly have won a world championship. I couldn't stand it. It seemed so unjust, and I broke out in big tears."

191
Joni Mitchell (1943-   )

"I always had star eyes, I think, [was] always interested in glamor",
the songwriter has recalled of her girlhood in Saskatoon. "I had one
very creative friend whom I played with a lot and we used to put
on circuses together, and he also played brilliant piano for his age
when he was a young boy. I used to dance around the room and
say that I was going to be a great ballerina and he was going to be
a great composer, or that he was going to be a great writer and I
was going to illustrate his books. My first experience with music
was at this boy's house, because he played the piano and they had
old instruments like autoharps lying around. It was playing his piano
that made me want to have one of my own to mess with, but then,
as soon as I expressed interest, they gave me lessons and that killed
it completely."

192
Michael Ondaatje (1943-   )

In a memoir of his childhood in what is now Sri Lanka, Ondaatje
writes: "I still believe the most beautiful alphabet was created by
the Sinhalese... The letters are washed blunt glass which betray no
jaggedness. Sanskrit was governed by verticals, but its sharp grid
features were not possible in Ceylon. Here the Ola leaves which
people wrote on were too brittle. A straight line would cut apart
the leaf and so a curling alphabet was derived from its Indian cousin."
These observations seem to have been prompted by the recollection

of how at "St Thomas' College Boys School I had written 'lines' as punishment." He gives examples, such as the sentence "I must not throw coconuts off the roof of Copplestone House" written out one hundred and fifty times. Another was: "We must not urinate again on Father Barnabus's tires." He explains: "A communal protest this time, the first of my socialist tendencies."

193
Neil Young (1945-   )

The singer's father, Scott Young, pays a visit to his son's home in California.

"One day Neil and I dropped into the big storage building where in 1981 he kept his two tour buses and some prime elements in his antique car collection—sixteen-cylinder Cadillacs, a 1934 Bentley, a La Salle, a Buick Roadmaster station wagon, the Packard station wagon... We wandered from there into a smaller storage area filled with scenery, his own travel trunks and some belonging to Joni Mitchell, boxes of...odds and ends...Also in the room were stacks of boxes full of records. 'You know what they are?' he asked. I didn't. '*Comes A Time* copies that were no good,' he said. The master tape of *Comes A Time* had been damaged. He checked it, thinking it wasn't quite right, but not able to identify what. So he okayed it. A week or so later he found one of the tapes taken off the original master. Checking the tape against the album, then ready, he found that some frequencies in the high register were missing altogether from the album. He called the Reprise people to say that production had to be stopped. Aghast, they said they had already printed and shipped

200,000 copies. He said it was his fault, and they must be recalled; he would pay for this personally. They told him it would cost $200,000, at one dollar per album plus shipping albums back from Italy and Japan where they'd been shipped. He said he would pay that.

"'I don't like throwing money around,' he said. 'But I wasn't going to have this album circulating around the world in bad quality.'

"'How do you make sure they won't get out sometime?'

"He showed me. Each case of albums had been fired at with a rifle, piercing each record and making it unusable."

194
Margaret Trudeau (1948-   )

In the sequel to her autobiography, describing her life as a media celebrity following the disintegration of her marriage to the prime minister, Margaret Trudeau recalled public incidents in which she defended him, as well as others in which she took rather the opposite tack. As Pierre Trudeau's popularity waned, opinionated taxi drivers began to affect her unduly. One Toronto cabby, unaware of his passenger's identity, went to far as to impugn Trudeau's sexual preferences and to suggest that his late marriage had been a sham. "Stop this cab", she piped up. "I don't have to sit and listen to you. You're an ugly, bigoted old man [and] I don't have to take rides from people like you. Never." Later, she began the international promotion tour for her book with a guest spot on the American television programme *Today*. Chatting idly before their live interview got underway, the show's host, Jane Pauley, remarked that her first name is actually Margaret and that she was about to marry Garry Trudeau, the political cartoonist. "You can have my name, with pleasure", her guest replied. "Take it for all the good it will do you. It's yours."

195
Karen Kain (1951-   )

The former dance critic of *The Globe and Mail,* writing about the crush he had on Kain:

"I went to her wedding at my own parish church with my beloved wife beside me. Miss Kain married a nice man whom I churlishly discounted that very morning in the newspaper, coming as close as I ever dared in print to tell her of the paragon she had rather nonchalantly passed by. She seemed happy, nonetheless, and my good mate understood. It was not infidelity I was about.

"Such purity of heart is not without its traps, for I was later told that Miss Kain can't stand people gushing over her and saying ridiculous things. Indeed, I believe that she first fell in love with her husband-to-be upon discovering that he hadn't a clue who she was."

196
Susan Musgrave (1951-   )

In 1986, the West Coast poet, whose work is known partly for its eroticism, arrived at a maximum security prison where she was scheduled to marry one of the inmates. She was dressed for the occasion in a purple dress with a moon and stars pattern in sequins. "It was criminally expensive, but you only get married for the third time once", she is quoted as saying. As she entered the reception area she passed an electronic weapons detector designed to register the presence of metal on a scale of from one to ten.

"You're a ten", a guard informed her.

"Why, thank you", she replied.

Her wedding garter had triggered the alarm.

197
Sheila Copps (1952-   )

The future Liberal MP first sought public office in the federal election of 1976, when she was twenty-four. A native gift for languages allowed her to speak Italian among the large Italian-Canadian population of Hamilton Centre and to exercise at least a phrase or two of Polish or Hungarian, as the situation seemed to warrant. To prepare for a Croatian dance, she memorized the Croation greeting *dobar dan hrvati*, which she was told meant "Good afternoon, people". In fact, the translation is "Good afternoon, Croation people". So the gesture was less well received the following day when she trotted it out at a Serbian picnic. The "potential voters visibly recoiled in horror", she later wrote. "My Serbian hosts were quick to hustle me off the stage and try to make amends. I didn't really understand their language, they explained. Later, a husky young Serbian man approached me and said I should thank my stars that I was a woman. Otherwise, I would have been taken out in the alley and assaulted."

There were six hundred eligible voters at the event. Copps lost the election by only sixteen votes.

198
Karen Magnussen (1952-   )

In 1965, Magnussen took part in a professional figure-skating competition for the first time. She did poorly—"something like twentieth in the first figure and thirteenth in the next, and I was fit to be tied", her coach, Linda Brauckmann recalled.

"I thought of all the hours and hours I'd used up on figures in the last year with that girl, and I saw it all going up in smoke. This has no similarity to what I knew she could do. So when she came off the ice after one of the figures, I just gave her hell...I asked her just who did she think she was?

"All around us people were turning and staring. The tears welled up in her eyes, and she toddled off into the dressing room. I found out later she had gone to her mother and said: 'Oh, Mother, Mrs. Brauckmann's upsetting me and I can't do my figures.' And her mother replied, 'Karen, I think it's probably you who's upsetting Mrs. Brauckmann.'"

The following year, Magnussen won her first Canadian women's figure skating championship.

199
Wayne Gretzky (1961-   )

Nelson Skalbania, the Vancouver entrepreneur, had never seen a live hockey game when he purchased the Edmonton Oilers in 1976. Nor had he ever seen Wayne Gretzky play when he flew him and his parents to the West Coast to negotiate the hockey prodigy's first professional contract, with Skalbania's second team, the Indianapolis Racers.

Skalbania, who is twenty years Gretzky's senior, had a novel way of making certain that the glowing reports submitted by talent scouts were not somehow mistaken. "We went on a six-mile run, and when he beat me, that was it", the businessman explained.

The agreement, extending seven years and valued at $1.75 million, was drawn up outdoors as the two runners were still perspiring from the race. Yet when Skalbania folded the Indiana team, he sold Gretzky's contract for only $250,000 to Peter Pocklington, who also acquired the Oilers. Pocklington promptly signed Gretzky to the longest term in professional sports history, twenty-one years.

At the end of his first season with Edmonton, Gretzky received an unexpected bonus, a black Ferrari worth $57,000. He was still only twenty years old.

In 1988, Pocklington sold him to Los Angeles.

Sources

1. *Champlain, The Life of Fortitude* by Morris Bishop. New York: Knopf, 1948.
2. *Amherst and Canada* by Louis des Cognets Jr. Princeton, New Jersey: the author, 1962.
3. *Guy Carleton, A Biography* by Paul R. Reynolds. Toronto: Gage Publishing, 1980.
4. *Journal of Captain John Knox.* Toronto: Champlain Society, 1906.
5. *Peter Porcupine, A Study of William Cobbett* by Marjorie Bowen. London: Longmans, Green, 1935.
6. *The Journals and Letters of Sir Alexander Mackenzie,* edited by W. Kaye Lamb. London: Cambridge University Press, 1970.
7. *The Life and Times of Wm. Lyon Mackenzie, with an Account of the Canadian Rebellion of 1837, and the Subsequent Frontier Disturbances, Chiefly from Unpublished Documents* by Charles Lindsey. Toronto: P.R. Randall, 1862.
8. *The Canadian Don Quixote: The Life and Works of Major John Richardson, Canada's First Novelist* by David R. Beasley. Erin, Ontario: Porcupine's Quill, 1977.
9. *Joseph Howe: Voice of Nova Scotia* edited by J. Murray Beck. Toronto: McClelland & Stewart, 1964.
10. *George-Etienne Cartier, Montreal Bourgeois* by Brian Young. Kingston and Montreal: McGill-Queen's University Press, 1981.
11. *Reminiscences Political and Personal* by Sir John Willison. Toronto: McClelland & Stewart, 1919.
12. *Brown of The Globe. Volume One: The Voice of Upper Canada 1818-1859* by J.M.S. Careless. Toronto: Macmillan of Canada, 1959.
13. *The Last Spike: The Great Railway 1881-1885* by Pierre Berton. Toronto: McClelland & Stewart, 1971.
14. *Reminiscences Political and Personal* by Sir John Willison. Toronto: McClelland & Stewart, 1919.
15. *Fifteen Men: Canada's Prime Ministers from Macdonald to Trudeau* by Gordon Donaldson. Toronto: Doubleday Canada, 1969.
16. *Candid Chronicles: Leaves from the Note Book of a Canadian Journalist* by Hector Charlesworth. Toronto: Macmillan of Canada, 1925.
17. *Amor De Cosmos, Journalist and Reformer* by George Woodcock. Toronto: Oxford University Press, 1975.
18. *The Molson Saga 1763-1983* by Shirley E. Woods Jr. Toronto: Doubleday Canada, 1983.
19. *Under the Studio Light, Leaves from a Portrait Painter's Sketch Book* by J.W.L. Forster. Toronto: Macmillan of Canada, 1928.
20. *Edward Blake* by Joseph Schull. Toronto: Macmillan of Canada, 1975-76.

21. *Under the Studio Light, Leaves from a Portrait Painter's Sketch Book* by J.W.L. Forster. Toronto: Macmillan of Canada, 1928.

22. Introduction by George Moreby Acklom to *Cosmic Consciousness, A Study of the Evolution of the Human Mind* by Richard Maurice Bucke. New York: E.P. Dutton, 1946.

23. *Diary of an Art Dealer* by René Gimpel, translated by John Rosenberg. London: Hamish Hamilton, 1986.

24. *Kootenai Brown, His Life and Times 1839-1916* by William Rodney. Sidney, B.C.: Gray's Publishing, 1969.

25. *Reminiscences Political and Personal* by Sir John Willison. Toronto: McClelland & Stewart, 1919.

26. *My Windows on the Street of the World* by James Mavor. London: J.M. Dent, 1923.

27. *David Boyle: From Artisan to Archaeologist* by Gerald Killan. Toronto: University of Toronto Press, 1983.

28. *Letters of Roger Fry,* edited by Denys Sutton. London: Chatto & Windus, 1972.

29. *Candid Chronicles: Leaves from the Note Book of a Canadian Journalist* by Hector Charlesworth. Toronto: Macmillan of Canada, 1925.

30. *Fifteen Men: Canada's Prime Ministers from Macdonald to Trudeau* by Gordon Donaldson. Toronto: Doubleday Canada, 1969.

31. *The Miracle of the Mountain: The Story of Brother André and the Shrine on Mount Royal* by Alden Hatch. New York: Hawthorn, 1959.

32. *Under the Studio Light, Leaves from a Portrait Painter's Sketch Book* by J.W.L. Forster. Toronto: Macmillan of Canada, 1928.

33. *Candid Chronicles: Leaves from the Note Book of a Canadian Journalist* by Hector Charlesworth. Toronto: Macmillan of Canada, 1925.

34. *Candid Chronicles: Leaves from the Note Book of a Canadian Journalist* by Hector Charlesworth. Toronto: Macmillan of Canada, 1925.

35. *More Candid Chronicles: Further Leaves from the Note Book of a Canadian Journalist* by Hector Charlesworth. Toronto: Macmillan of Canada, 1928.

36. *The Doctor Who Dared: William Osler* by Iris Noble. Toronto: Copp Clark, 1959.

37. *More Candid Chronicles: Further Leaves from the Note Book of a Canadian Journalist* by Hector Charlesworth. Toronto: Macmillan of Canada, 1928.

38. *Persons, Papers and Things* by Paul Bilkey. Toronto: Ryerson Press, 1940.

39. *Sons of Canada, Short Studies of Characteristic Canadians* by Augustus Bridle. Toronto: J.M. Dent, 1916.

40. *My Windows on the Street of the World* by James Mavor. London: J. M. Dent, 1923.

41. *Canadian Portraits: Famous Women* by Byrne Hope Sanders. Toronto: Clarke, Irwin, 1958.

42. *Flame of Power* by Peter C. Newman (Toronto: McClelland & Stewart, 1959) and *Fair Dinkum* by David M. Legate (Toronto: Doubleday Canada, 1969).

43. *Reminiscences Political and Personal* by Sir John Willison. Toronto: McClelland & Stewart, 1919.

44. *The Private Capital: Ambition and Love in the Age of Macdonald and Laurier* by Sandra Gwyn. Toronto: McClelland & Stewart, 1984.

45. *A Canadian Millionaire: The Life and Business Times of Sir Joseph Flavelle, Bart., 1858-1939*, by Michael Bliss. Toronto: Macmillan of Canada, 1978.

46. *Memory Hold-the-Door* by John Buchan. Toronto: Musson, 1941.

47. *Memory's Wall, The Autobiography of Flora McCrea Eaton* by Flora McCrea Eaton. Toronto: Clarke, Irwin, 1956.

48. *In My Time: A Memoir*, by Thomas H. Raddall. Toronto: McClelland & Stewart, 1976.

49. *Candid Chronicles: Leaves from the Note Book of a Canadian Journalist* by Hector Charlesworth. Toronto: Macmillan of Canada, 1925.

50. *More Candid Chronicles: Further Leaves from the Note Book of a Canadian Journalist* by Hector Charlesworth. Toronto: Macmillan of Canada, 1928.

51. *Brave Harvest, The Life Story of E. Cora Hind, LL.D.* by Kennethe M. Haig. Toronto: Thomas Allen, 1945.

52. *Sons of Canada, Short Studies of Characteristic Canadians* by Augustus Bridle. Toronto: J.M. Dent, 1916.

53. *Pauline, A Biography of Pauline Johnson* by Betty Keller. Vancouver: Douglas & McIntyre, 1981. Reissued Halifax: Formac Publishing, 1987.

54. *Variety Show: Twenty Years of Watching the News Parade* by Frederick Griffin. Toronto: Macmillan of Canada, 1936. See also *A Concise History of Capital Punishment in Canada* by Frank W. Anderson. Calgary: Frontier Publishing, 1973.

55. *The Fabulous Kelley, Canada's King of the Medicine Men* by Thomas P. Kelley Jr. Toronto: Simon & Schuster of Canada, 1974.

56. *Henry Marshall Tory, Beloved Canadian* by E.A. Corbett. Toronto: Ryerson Press, 1954.

57. *Debrett's Illustrated Guide to the Canadian Establishment*, edited by Peter C. Newman. Toronto: Methuen, 1983.

58. *Duff: A Life in the Law* by David Ricardo Williams. Toronto: Osgoode Society, 1984.

59. *Dafoe of the Free Press* by Murray Donnelly. Toronto: Macmillan of Canada, 1968.

60. *Canadian Portraits: Famous Women* by Byrne Hope Sanders. Toronto: Clarke, Irwin, 1958.

61. *Oscar Wilde* by Richard Ellmann (New York: Knopf, 1988) and *Oscar Wilde, A Biography* by H. Montgomnery Hyde (New York: Farrar, Straus and Giroux, 1975).

62. *Remembering Leacock*, edited by Allan Anderson. Toronto: Deneau, 1983.

63. *Eye Opener Bob: The Story of Bob Edwards* by Grant MacEwan. Edmonton: Institute of Applied Arts, 1957.

64. *Recollections of People, Press, and Politics* by Grattan O'Leary. Toronto: Macmillan of Canada, 1977.

65. *I'm Telling You, Being the Further Candid Chronicles of Hector Charlesworth* by Hector Charlesworth. Toronto: Macmillan of Canada, 1937.

66. *Emily Carr as I Knew Her* by Carol Pearson. Toronto: Clarke, Irwin, 1954.

67. *Candid Chronicles: Leaves from the Note Book of a Canadian Journalist* by Hector Charlesworth. Toronto: Macmillan of Canada, 1925.

68. *I'm Telling You, Being the Further Candid Chronicles of Hector Charlesworth* by Hector Charlesworth. Toronto: Macmillan of Canada, 1937.

69. *The Stream Runs Fast, My Own Story* by Nellie L. McClung. Toronto: Thomas Allen, 1945.

70. *A Very Double Life, The Private World of Mackenzie King* by C.P. Stacey. Toronto: Macmillan of Canada, 1976.

71. *Persons, Papers and Things* by Paul Bilkey. Toronto: Ryerson Press, 1940.

72. *Fifteen Men: Canada's Prime Ministers from Macdonald to Trudeau* by Gordon Donaldson. Toronto: Doubleday Canada, 1969.

73. *Why Not Grow Young? Or Living for Longevity* by Robert W. Service. London: Ernest Benn, 1928.

74. *Mr. Buchan, Writer: A Life of the First Lord Tweedsmuir* by Arthur C. Turner. Toronto: Macmillan of Canada, 1949.

75. *Something Hidden, A Biography of Wilder Penfield* by Jefferson Lewis. Toronto: Doubleday Canada, 1981.

76. *Sir Arthur Currie, A Biography* by Daniel G. Dancocks. Toronto: Methuen, 1985.

77. *The Tom Thomson Mystery* by William T. Little. Toronto: McGraw-Hill, 1970.

78. *Both Sides of the Street: One Man's Life in Business and the Arts in Canada* by Floyd S. Chalmers. Toronto: Macmillan of Canada, 1983.

79. *The Beaverbrook I Knew,* edited by Logan Gourlay (London: Quartet Books, 1984) and *Beaverbrook* by A.J.P. Taylor (London: Hamish Hamilton, 1972).

80. *Mazo de la Roche of Jalna* by Ronald Hambleton. Toronto: General Publishing, 1966.

81. *Ernest Jones, Freud's Alter Ego* by Vincent Brome. New York: W.W. Norton, 1983.

82. *Stef: A Biography of Vilhjalmur Stefansson, Canadian Arctic Explorer* by William R. Hunt. Vancouver: University of British Columbia Press, 1986.

83. *Variety Show: Twenty Years of Watching the News Parade* by Frederick Griffin. Toronto: Macmillan of Canada, 1936.

84. *Elizabeth Bagshaw* by Marjorie Wild. Toronto: Fitzhenry & Whiteside, 1984.

85. *Memory's Wall, The Autobiography of Flora McCrea Eaton* by Flora McCrea Eaton. Toronto: Clarke, Irwin, 1956.

86. *The Other A.Y. Jackson, A Memoir* by O.J. Firestone. Toronto: McClelland & Stewart, 1979.

87. *A Very Public Life. Volume I: Far From Home* by Paul Martin. Ottawa: Deneau Publishers, 1983.

88. *A Slice of Canada: Memoirs* by Watson Kirkconnell. Toronto: University of Toronto Press, 1967.

89. *Louis St. Laurent, Canadian* by Dale C. Thompson. Toronto: Macmillan of Canada, 1967.

90. *A Canadian for All Seasons: The John E. Robbins Story* by John A.B. McLeish. Toronto: Lester & Orpen, 1978.

91. *Canada's Mystery Man of High Finance: The Story of Izaak Walton Killam and His Glittering Wife Dorothy* by Douglas How. Hantsport, Nova Scotia: Lancelot Press, 1986.

92. *C.D. Howe, A Biography* by Robert Bothwell and William Kilbourn. Toronto: McClelland & Stewart, 1979.

93. *Born in a Bookshop* by Vincent Starrett. Norman: University of Oklahoma Press, 1965.

94. *A Hundred Different Lives, An Autobiography* by Raymond Massey. Toronto: McClelland & Stewart, 1979.

95. *Bright Glass of Memory, A Set of Four Memoirs* by Douglas LePan. Toronto: McGraw-Hill Ryerson, 1979.

96. *Devil in Deerskins: My Life with Grey Owl* by Anahareo. Toronto: New Press, 1972.

97. *The Making of a Peacemonger: The Memoirs of George Ignatieff* by George Ignatieff with Sonja Sinclair. Toronto: University of Toronto Press, 1985.

98. *The Life and Times of General Two-Gun Cohen* by Charles Drage. New York: Funk & Wagnalls, 1954.

99. *Frank H. Underhill, Intellectual Provocateur* by R. Douglas Francis. Toronto: University of Toronto Press, 1986.

100. *Bethune* by Roderick Stewart. Toronto: New Press, 1973.

101. *Louis St. Laurent, Canadian* by Dale C. Thomson. Toronto: Macmillan of Canada, 1967.

102. *Least of All Saints: The Story of Aimee Semple McPherson* by Robert Bahr. Englewood Cliffs, New Jersey: Prentice Hall, 1979.

103. *Notebooks* by Thoreau MacDonald. Moonbeam, Ontario: Penumbra Press, 1980.

104. *Plain Talk! Memoirs of an Auditor General* by Maxwell Henderson. Toronto: McClelland & Stewart, 1984.

105. *Variety Show: Twenty Years of Watching the News Parade* by Frederick Griffin. Toronto: Macmillan of Canada, 1936.

106. *Mayor of All the People* by Nathan Phillips. Toronto: McClelland & Stewart, 1967.

107. *Sweetheart, The Story of Mary Pickford* by Robert Windeler. New York: Praeger, 1973.

108. *The Courage of the Early Morning: A Son's Biography of a Famous Father* by William Arthur Bishop. Toronto: McClelland & Stewart, 1965.

109. *Harold Adams Innis, Portrait of a Scholar* by Donald Creighton (Toronto: University of Toronto Press, 1957) and *A Date with History: Memoirs of a Canadian Historian* by C.P. Stacey (Ottawa: Deneau, 1983).

110. *Storm Signals, More Undiplomatic Diaries, 1962-1971* by Charles Ritchie. Toronto: Macmillan of Canada, 1983.

111. *One Canada, Memoirs of the Right Honourable John G. Diefenbaker: The Crusading Years 1895-1956* by John Diefenbaker. Toronto: Macmillan of Canada, 1975.

112. *The News Game* by Roy Greenaway. Toronto: Clarke, Irwin, 1966.

113. *A Man Called Intrepid* by William Stevenson. New York: Harcourt Brace Jovanovich, 1976.

114. *A Very Public Life. Volume II: So Many Worlds* by Paul Martin. Toronto: Deneau Publishers, 1985.

115. *Both Sides of the Street: One Man's Life in Business and the Arts in Canada* by Floyd S. Chalmers. Toronto: Macmillan of Canada, 1983.

116. *The News Game* by Roy Greenaway. Toronto: Clarke, Irwin, 1966.

117. *Helen Creighton: A Life in Folklore* by Helen Creighton. Toronto: McGraw-Hill Ryerson, 1974.

118. "Charles E. Feinberg: Book Collector" by William White. *The Private Library* (London), Summer 1968.

119. *Debrett's Illustrated Guide to the Canadian Establishment,* edited by Peter C. Newman. Toronto: Methuen, 1983.

120. *The Politics of the Imagination: A Life of F.R. Scott* by Sandra Djwa. Toronto: McClelland & Stewart, 1987.

121. *Shovelling Trouble* by Mordecai Richler. Toronto: McClelland & Stewart, 1972.

122. *Will the Real Gordon Sinclair Please Stand Up* by Gordon Sinclair. Toronto: McClelland & Stewart, 1966. "Farewell to a cherished curmudgeon", *Maclean's,* May 28, 1984.

123. *Years of Choice 1960-1968* by Gérard Pelletier, translated by Alan Brown. Toronto: Methuen, 1987.

124. *How I Earned $250,000 as a Free Lance Writer ... Even If It Did Take Me 30 Years!* by Ronald Hambleton. Toronto: Bartholomew Green, 1977.

125. "Introduction" by Ramsay Derry to *The Passionate Observer: Selected Writings* by Donald Creighton. Toronto: McClelland & Stewart, 1980.

126. *How I Earned $250,000 as a Free Lance Writer ... Even If It Did Take Me 30 Years!* by Ronald Hambleton. Toronto: Bartholomew Green, 1977.

127. *A Very Public Life. Volume I: Far from Home* by Paul Martin. Ottawa: Deneau Publishers, 1983.

128. *In My Time: A Memoir* by Thomas H. Raddall. Toronto: McClelland & Stewart, 1976.

129. *The Great Scot: A Biography of Donald Gordon* by Joseph Schull. Montreal: McGill-Queen's University Press, 1979.

130. *The Making of a Socialist: The Recollections of T.C. Douglas,* edited by Lewis H. Thomas. Edmonton: University of Alberta Press, 1982.

131. *The Other A.Y. Jackson, A Memoir* by O.J. Firestone. Toronto: McClelland & Stewart, 1979.

132. *A Political Memoir* by Walter L. Gordon. Toronto: McClelland & Stewart, 1977.

133. *Andrew Allan, A Self-Portrait,* edited by Harry J. Boyle. Toronto: Macmillan of Canada, 1974.

134. *Hugh MacLennan, A Writer's Life* by Elspeth Cameron. Toronto: University of Toronto Press, 1981.

135. *Anne Francis, An Autobiography* by Florence Bird. Toronto: Clarke, Irwin, 1974.

136. *A Life in Our Times: Memoirs* by John Kenneth Galbraith. Boston: Houghton Mifflin, 1981.

137. *In Search of Greatness* by Yousuf Karsh. Toronto: University of Toronto Press, 1962.

138. *Stanley Knowles: The Man from Winnipeg North Centre* by Susan Mann Trofimenkoff. Saskatoon: Western Producer Books, 1982.

139. *Sinc, Betty, and the Morning Man: The Story of CFRB* by Donald Jack. Toronto: Macmillan of Canada, 1977.

140. *Waterfront Warlord: The Life and Violent Times of Hal C. Banks* by Peter Edwards. Toronto: Key Porter Books, 1987.

141. *Being Geniuses Together 1920-1930* by Robert McAlmon, revised and with supplementary chapters by Kay Boyle. London: Michael Joseph, 1970.

142. *Malcolm Lowry: Vancouver Days* by Sheryl Salloum. Vancouver: Harbour Publishing, 1987.

143. *Take a Chance! Confessions of a Quizmaster* by Roy Ward Dickson. Toronto: Fitzhenry & Whiteside, 1977.

144. *Theatrical Anecdotes* by Peter Hay. New York: Oxford University Press, 1987.

145. *One Damn Thing After Another!* by Hugh Garner. Toronto: McGraw-Hill Ryerson, 1979.

146. *Irving Layton: A Portrait* by Elspeth Cameron. Toronto: Stoddart Publishing, 1985.

147. *The Dark Broad Seas, Memoirs of a Sailor. Vol. 1: With Many Voices* by Jeffry V. Brock. Toronto: McClelland & Stewart, 1981.

148. *One Damn Thing After Another!* by Hugh Garner. Toronto: McGraw-Hill Ryerson, 1973.

149. *The Making of a Peacemonger, The Memoirs of George Ignatieff* by George Ignatieff with Sonja Sinclair. Toronto: University of Toronto Press, 1985.

150. *Paper Boy* by Stuart Keate. Toronto: Clarke, Irwin, 1980.

151. *The Boyd Gang* by Marjorie Lamb and Barry Pearson. Toronto: Peter Martin Associates, 1976.

152. *Gentlemen, Players and Politicians* by Dalton Camp. Toronto: McClelland & Stewart, 1970.

153. *An Anecdotal Memoir* by Charles Templeton. Toronto: McClelland & Stewart, 1983.

154. *Les Girls* by Constance Tomkinson. Boston: Little, Brown, 1956.

155. *Drapeau* by Brian McKenna and Susan Purcell. Toronto: Clarke, Irwin, 1980.

156. *How I Earned $250,000 as a Free Lance Writer ... Even If It Did Take Me 30 Years!* by Ronald Hambleton. Toronto: Bartholomew Green, 1977.

157. *Looking for Trouble* by Peter Worthington. Toronto: Key-Porter Books, 1984.

158. *Memoirs of a Literary Blockhead* by Robin Skelton. Toronto: Macmillan of Canada, 1988.

159. *Radical Tories: The Conservative Tradition in Canada* by Charles Taylor. Toronto: Anansi, 1982.

160. *A Very Public Life. Volume II: So Many Worlds* by Paul Martin. Toronto: Deneau Publishers, 1985.

161. *One Damn Thing After Another!* by Hugh Garner. Toronto: McGraw-Hill Ryerson, 1979.

162. *Years of Choice 1960-1968* by Gérard Pelletier, translated by Alan Brown. Toronto: Methuen, 1987.

163. *Points of Departure* by Dalton Camp. Ottawa: Deneau & Greenberg, 1979.

164. *Theatrical Anecdotes* by Peter Hay. New York: Oxford University Press, 1987.

165. *Oh, What a Blow That Phantom Gave Me!* by Edmund Carpenter. New York: Holt, Rinehart and Winston, 1973.

166. *Memoirs* by René Lévesque, translated by Philip Stratford. Toronto: McClelland & Stewart, 1986.

167. "Hereafter known as the party of the first part" by Val Clery, *Quill & Quire,* April 1985.

168. *Her Excellency Jeanne Sauvé* by Shirley E. Woods. Toronto: Macmillan of Canada, 1986.

169. "Pontificial Institute Loses Father Boyle", University of Toronto *Graduate,* November-December 1984.

170. *Both Sides of the Street: One Man's Life in Business and the Arts in Canada,* by Floyd S. Chalmers. Toronto: Macmillan of Canada, 1983.

171. *Looking for Trouble* by Peter Worthington. Toronto: Key-Porter Books, 1984.

172. *And Now ... Here's Max* by Max Ferguson. Toronto: McGraw-Hill, 1967.

173. *Memoirs of a Bird in a Gilded Cage* by Judy LaMarsh. Toronto: McClelland & Stewart, 1969.

174. "A man who could well be called intrepid", *Maclean's,* November 3, 1980.

175. Obituaries in *The Globe and Mail,* June 2, 1987, and *The Toronto Star,* June 3, 1987.

176. *Theatrical Anecdotes* by Peter Hay. New York: Oxford University Press, 1987.

177. *Sinc, Betty, and the Morning Man: The Story of CFRB* by Donald Jack. Toronto: Macmillan of Canada, 1977.

178. *Margaret Laurence, An Appreciation* edited by Christl Verduyn. Peterborough, Ontario: Broadview Press, 1988.

179. *Telling Tales* by John Fraser. Toronto: Collins, 1986.

180. *Pattison, Portrait of a Capitalist Superstar* by Russell Kelly. Vancouver: New Star Books, 1986.

181. *Have I Ever Lied to You Before?* by Jerry Goodis. Toronto: McClelland & Stewart, 1972.

182. *Telling Tales* by John Fraser. Toronto: Collins, 1986.

183. "An old-fashioned dandy who left a mark" by Robert Fulford, Toronto *Star,* October 11, 1986.

184. *Six Journeys: A Canadian Pattern* by Charles Taylor. Toronto: Anansi, 1977.

185. *Telling Tales* by John Fraser. Toronto: Collins, 1986.

186. *As It Happened* by Barbara Frum. Toronto: McClelland & Stewart, 1976.

187. *My Story* by Tommy Hunter with Liane Heller. Toronto: Methuen, 1985.

188. *Honourable Mentions—The Uncommon Diary of an M.P.* by Roy MacLaren. Toronto: Deneau, 1986.

189. *Mulroney: The Making of the Prime Minister* by L. Ian MacDonald. Toronto: McClelland & Stewart, 1984.

190. *Nancy Greene, An Autobiography* by Nancy Greene and Jack Batten. Don Mills: General Publishing, 1969.

191. *Joni Mitchell* by Leonore Fleischer. New York: Flash Books, 1976.

192. *Running in the Family* by Michael Ondaatje. Toronto: McClelland & Stewart, 1983.

193. *Neil and Me* by Scott Young. Toronto: McClelland & Stewart, 1984.

194. *Consequences* by Margaret Trudeau. Toronto: Bantam Books, 1982.

195. *Telling Tales* by John Fraser. Toronto: Collins, 1986.

196. "Songs of the Sea-Witch" by John Goddard, *Saturday Night,* July 1987.

197. *Nobody's Baby* by Sheila Copps. Toronto: Deneau, 1986.

198. *Karen: The Karen Magnussen Story* by Karen Magnussen and Jeff Cross. Toronto: Collier-Macmillan of Canada, 1973.

199. *The Canadian Establishment, Vol. Two: The Acquisitors* by Peter C. Newman. Toronto: McClelland & Stewart, 1981.

Index of Persons

(page references are to anecdote numbers)